DETROIT PUBLIC LIBRARY
P9-DBT-962

# Smart Science Tricks

**Martin Gardner**

illustrated by

**Bob Steimle**

Sterling Publishing Co., Inc.
New York

### *More Puzzles and Tricks from Martin Gardner*

*Classic Brainteasers*
*Mental Magic*
*Mind-Boggling Word Puzzles*
*Science Tricks / Science Magic*

### *Acknowledgments*

I wish to thank *Physics Teacher* for permission to reprint my "Trick of the Month" feature, and Sterling's Sheila Anne Barry for expert editing and handling of the book's production. Thanks too to Glen Vecchione, for his masterly assistance with the science explanations.

To Jerry Andrus, magician and friend,
whose original optical illusions
have broken amazing new pathways.

Library of Congress Cataloging-in-Publication Data Available

10 9 8 7 6 5 4 3 2 1

Published by Sterling Publishing Co., Inc.
387 Park Avenue South, New York, NY 10016

Distributed in Canada by Sterling Publishing
c/o Canadian Manda Group, 165 Dufferin Street
Toronto, Ontario, Canada M6K 3H6
Distributed in Great Britain and Europe by Chris Lloyd
at Orca Book Services, Stanley House, Fleets Lane,
Poole BH15 3AJ, England
Distributed in Australia by Capricorn Link (Australia) Pty. Ltd.
P.O. Box 704, Windsor, NSW 2756, Australia

*Printed in China*


Sterling ISBN 1-4027-0910-2 Hardcover
ISBN 1-4027-2220-6 Paperback

# CONTENTS

## To Parents and Teachers

SIR DAVID BREWSTER, A FAMOUS NINETEENTH-CENTURY Scottish physicist, wrote a book in 1856 titled *The Stereoscope: Its History, Theory, and Construction*. Brewster did not invent the stereoscope, but he greatly improved it. Chapter XIV, on amusing ways to use a stereoscope, opens with the following paragraph:

> *Every experiment in science, and every instrument depending on scientific principles, when employed for the purpose of amusement, must necessarily be instructive. "Philosophy in sport" never fails to become "Science in earnest." The toy which amuses the child will instruct the sage, and many an eminent discoverer and inventor can trace the pursuits which immortalize them to some experiment or instrument which amused them at school. The soap bubbles, the kite, the balloon, the water wheel, the sundial, the burning glass, the magnet . . . have all been valuable incentives to the study of the sciences.*

About half the tricks in this book appeared as "Physics Trick of the Month" in *Physics Teacher*, a periodical that has long stressed the educational value of recreational science. Most of these tricks were reprinted as "Gardner's Corner" in the handsome magazine *Magic*. The other half of the items in the present book appear here for the first time.

## Before You Begin

HERE ARE CLOSE TO A HUNDRED TRICKS, PUZZLES, ILLUSIONS, and amusing experiments that you can do at home. They are all amazing; they are all fun, and with few exceptions they make use of items and materials you probably already have around the house.

If you see a hand symbol like the one at the right next to a trick, it means that if you are very young, you will need an adult to assist you because the trick requires potentially dangerous things, such as candles, matches, nails, and so on.

If you know of any science amusement that is not in this book or its predecessor, *Science Magic* (published in hardcover by Sterling in 1997, and issued as a paperback titled *Science Tricks* the next year), I would enjoy hearing about it. You can reach me with a letter in care of Sterling.

I hope you like the tricks!

—Martin Gardner

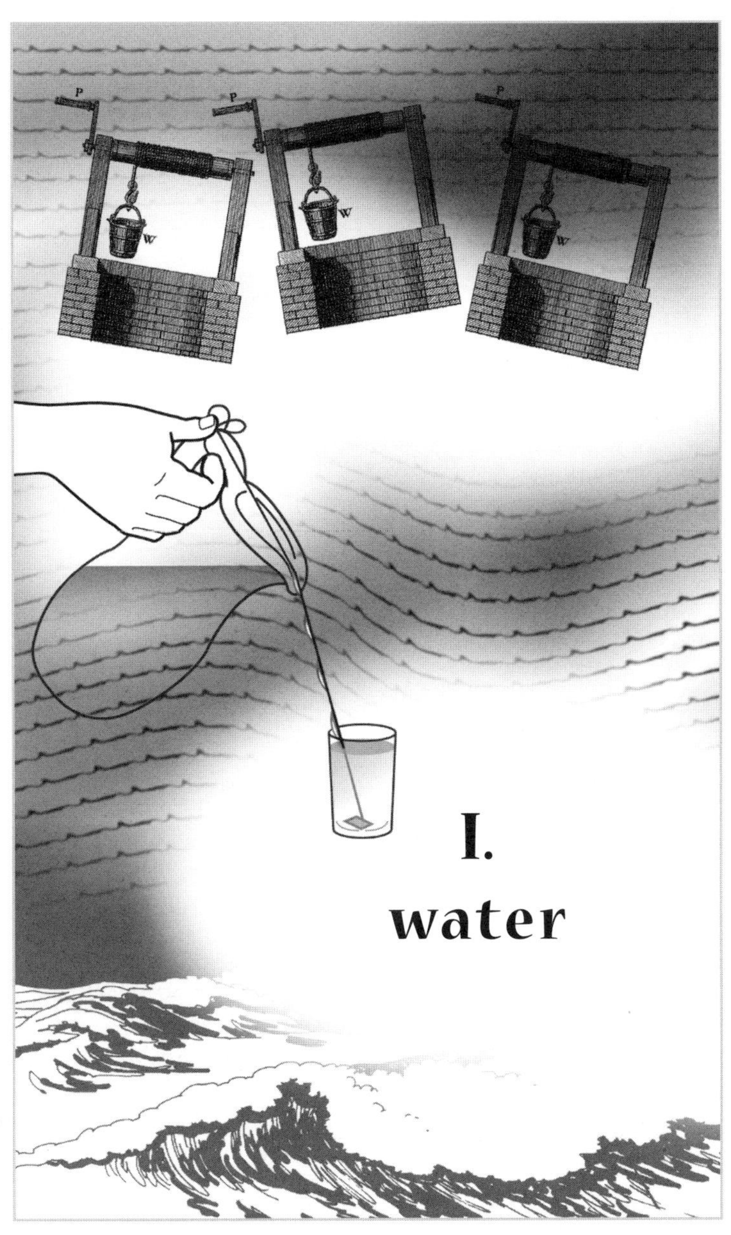


# I. water

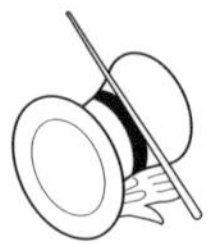

# 1

# REVERSE JACK'S PROFILE

**You need:**

- the jack of spades or the jack of hearts from a deck of cards
- glass of water
- clear swizzle stick or transparent glass or plastic rod
- paper and pencil

A PLAYING CARD JACK MYSTERIOUSLY DOES AN ABOUT-FACE, and a stirring rod alters the meaning of a sentence.

There are two one-eyed jacks in a deck of cards: the jack of spades and the jack of hearts. Hold either one behind a glass of water. If you press the Jack against the side of the glass and view him through the water, he will face in his normal direction as printed on the card. Move the card slowly away from the glass, and you'll see jack turn around and face the other way.

Take a transparent glass or plastic rod or a clear swizzle stick and hold it slightly above the short statement "bob KICKED pop," and you'll see what "pop" did next.

why?

## Why does it work?

A glass can act like a cylindrical lens. It reverses what is seen through it. The transparent rod is also a cylindrical lens. When held horizontally over print, it turns letters upside down. The letters of "KICKED" are the same when upside-down-reversed. And of course, this is also true of "O." On the contrary, the letter "p" becomes a "b" when inverted; a "b" turns into a "p."

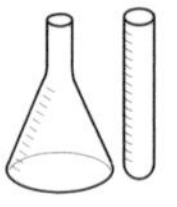

# 2 ZERO GRAVITY

### You need:

empty plastic bottle ✓
sharp pencil ✓

HERE'S A SIMPLE WAY TO DEMONSTRATE THAT GRAVITY vanishes inside a freely falling container. (I recommend that you perform this stunt outdoors over the grass.)

With a sharp pencil, make two holes on opposite sides of a plastic bottle, near the bottom. With your thumb and finger over the holes, fill the container with water. If you remove your thumb and finger, gravity will of course cause the water to run out through the holes.

However, if you hold the bottle high and let go, the bottle will fall, of course, but no water will escape. It is a good model of a spacecraft in free fall as it orbits Earth.

Why?

### Why does it work?

In a gravitational field, everything falls at the same speed, regardless of its weight or what it's made of. In this

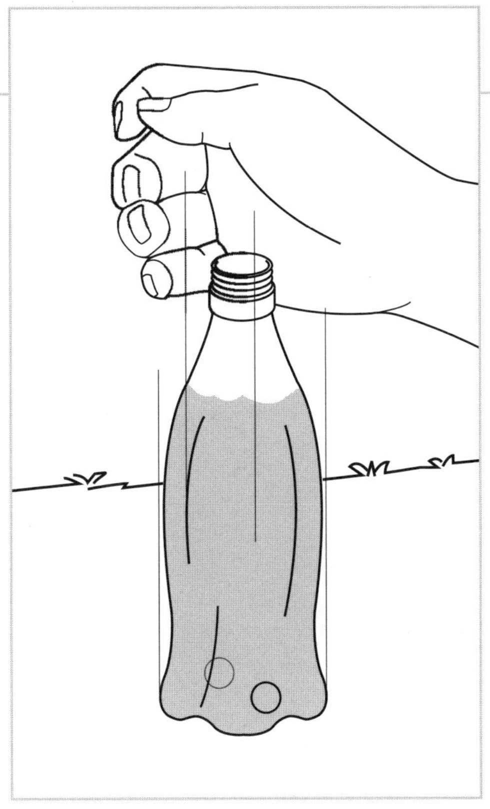

experiment, the water and the plastic bottle both fall at the same speed, so the water doesn't leak out. In a spacecraft in circular orbit around Earth, everything inside the spacecraft is, in effect, falling toward Earth at the same speed. So if you were in the spacecraft and let go of the bottle of water, it would stay put, right where you let go of it, and the water wouldn't leak out, because you, the bottle, and the water are all falling at the same speed.

# 3

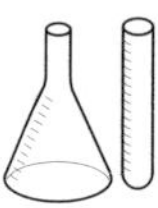

# ARCHIMEDES' PUMP

**You need:**

- rubber tube
- rod or piece of pipe
- duct tape or masking tape
- 2 bowls

ARCHIMEDES, THE GREEK MATHematician, is said to have invented this simple way to pump water to a higher level. It was actually widely used in ancient times.

Wrap a rubber tube around a rod or piece of pipe, fastening it down with tape, as shown. When you place the lower end of the pipe or rod in a bowl of water and rotate it, the water will travel up the tube to flow out the upper end into a basin or bowl held below it.

## Why does it work?

Water flows to the lower part of each coil. As the helix rotates, these water-bearing coils are carried upward to dump their water when they reach the top.

# 4

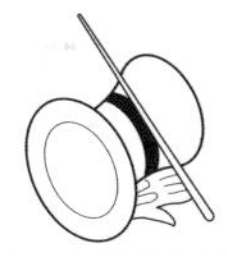

# THE WATER KNOT

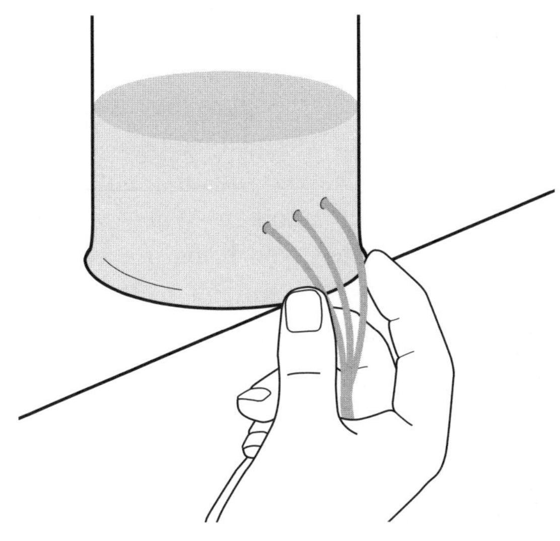

THREE STREAMS OF WATER MAGICALLY blend into a single stream and separate again when you run a finger over them.

You need:

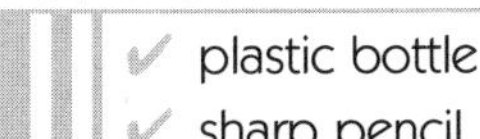
- plastic bottle
- sharp pencil

Near the bottom of a plastic bottle, use a sharp pencil to punch three small holes side by side, with about a quarter of an inch between them. When you fill the bottle with water, three streams will emerge from the holes.

With your finger and thumb, pinch the streams together. They will form a single stream. Now run your finger across the holes. The streams will separate again.

## Why does it work?

Water molecules are shaped in such a way that one side has a negative charge and the other, a positive charge. The negatively charged side of one molecule attracts the positively charged side of another molecule so that they stick to one another. When you pinch the streams of water together, you bring the molecules from the different streams close enough so that they adhere. When you run your finger across the holes, you interrupt the streams momentarily. When the water starts to flow, the molecules in different streams are once again too far apart to attract each other.

# 5

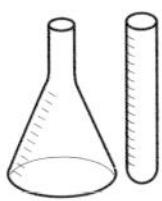

# A PEBBLE CURIOSITY

A GLASS FILLED WITH LARGE MARBLES seems to have more empty spaces inside it than a glass filled with small marbles. Which glass has the larger volume of empty space?

For this experiment you can use a supply of marbles of two different sizes, but any small spheres will do also, such as round balls of bubble gum and other kinds of candy.

Assuming you are using marbles, fill a glass to the brim with the small marbles and fill another glass to the brim with the larger marbles. Next, fill one of the glasses with water. Now pour the water from that glass into the second glass. You will find that both glasses hold the same amount of water.

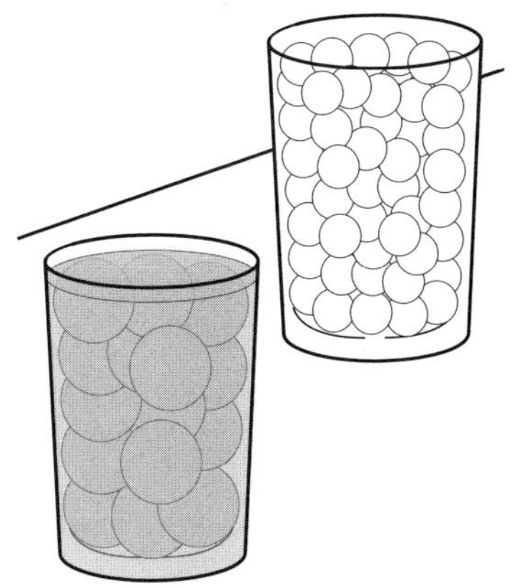

## Why does it work?

A full explanation would involve complicated solid geometry. The large marbles have bigger spaces between them. The glass with the smaller marbles has smaller spaces, but a lot more of them.

# 6

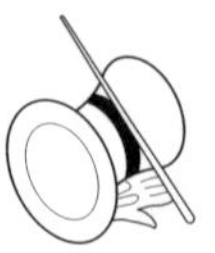

# WATER DOWN THE STRING

**You need:**

- a foot-long (30cm) piece of string ✓
- glass of water ✓
- small pitcher ✓

DID YOU KNOW THAT WATER WILL RUN DOWN A STRING AS IF the string is a tube?

Soak the string in water. Tie one end of it to the pitcher, which is half-filled with water. Pull the string taut over the spout of the pitcher, as shown. Tape the other end of the string to the inside of a glass. While keeping the string taut, slowly tilt the pitcher. The water will run down the string and into the glass.

## Why does it work?

Water molecules stick to each other, and you can see this when you pour water out of a pitcher—the water comes out in a stream rather than in chunks. Normally,

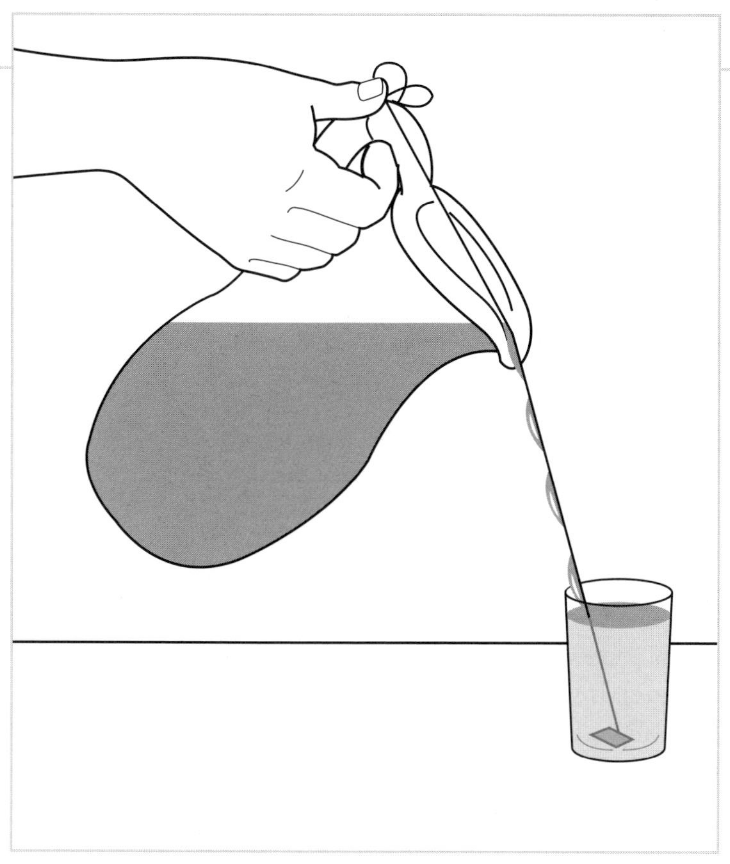

the water molecules follow the pull of gravity straight down. When you add the wet string and you pour slowly enough, the water trickles down the string. This happens because the attraction of the water molecules for each other is greater than the force of gravity, which would pull them straight down. The string itself also attracts water molecules, because its woven fibers create a lot of small spaces for the water to get into.

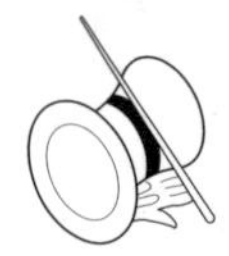

# 7

# THE BEAUTIFUL EGG

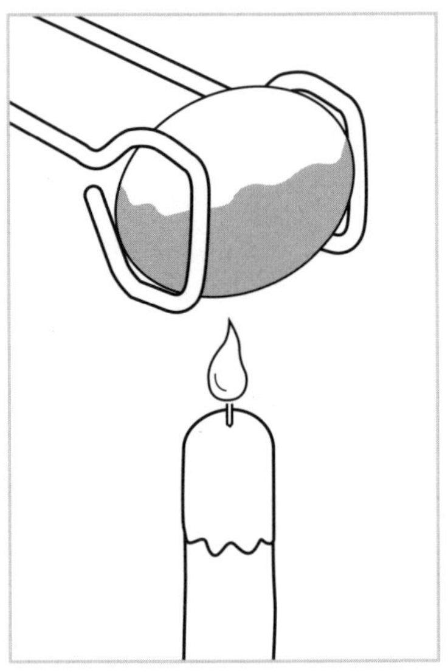

YOU CAN MAKE AN EGG look as if it's made of silver!

Place the egg in a spoon and hold it over a candle flame until it is completely covered with black soot. Then soak it in water. It will take on a beautiful silver appearance.

Why?

You need:

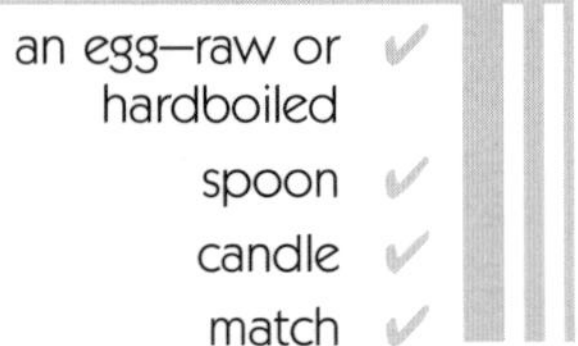

- an egg—raw or hardboiled
- spoon
- candle
- match

## Why does it work?

The silver effect is created by thousands of tiny bubbles that form at the sooty surface of the egg. This is because the carbon in the soot repels the water and creates the bubbles. The bubbles are so small that you can't see them very clearly, but they reflect light back to your eyes and make the egg's shell appear silver.

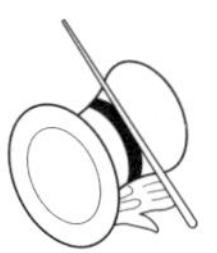

# 8

# THE MYSTERIOUS EGG

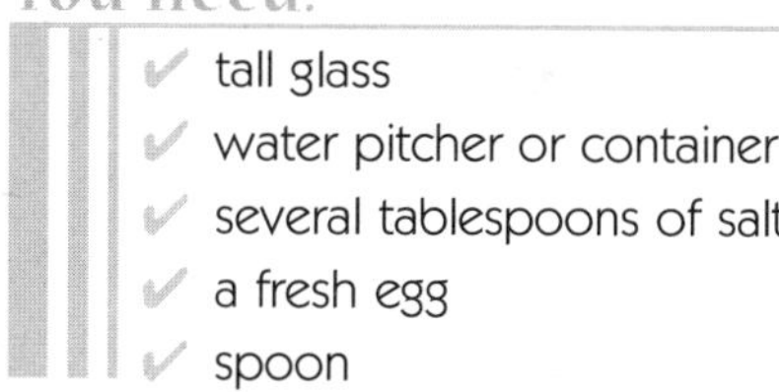

**You need:**

- ✔ tall glass
- ✔ water pitcher or container
- ✔ several tablespoons of salt
- ✔ a fresh egg
- ✔ spoon

IT SEEMS IMPOSSIBLE FOR AN EGG TO FLOAT HALFWAY DOWN a full glass of water, but you can achieve this easily!

Fill a tall glass half full of water. Add several tablespoons of salt and stir until the salt is thoroughly dissolved.

A fresh egg will float on the surface.

Now hold a spoon on the surface and carefully pour fresh water over it, using the bowl of the spoon to spread the water gently over the salt solution.

Result? An egg floating mysteriously in the middle of a glass that seems to hold just ordinary water. Put the glass on a shelf or mantel as a curiosity to baffle visitors.

### Why does it work?

The salt raises the specific gravity or density in the lower half of the glass. This is sufficient to allow the egg to float. Because the water in the upper part of the glass remains unsalted, the floating egg will not rise through it.

# 9

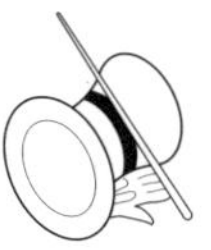

# THE MAGIC GLASS

**You need:**

- shot glass with cone-shaped interior
- transparent glass marble
- transparent glue
- black paint
- small picture
- water

FOR THIS NOVEL TRICK, YOU NEED A SPECIAL GLASS—A THICK-sided glass jigger (shot glass) with a cone-shaped interior. Place the marble inside the glass and glue it firmly in place. Paste the small picture on the outside bottom of the glass, photo side up, and paint the bottom black to conceal the fact that a picture is there.

Look down into the glass. You see nothing. Fill it with water, and the magnified picture appears like magic!

## Why does this work?

In the air, the glass sphere acts as a convex lens with a very long focal length. Surrounding the sphere with water greatly decreases its focal length, allowing it to behave like an ordinary magnifying glass that shows the picture in focus.

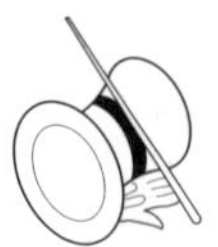

# 10

# THE MYSTERIOUS SIPHON

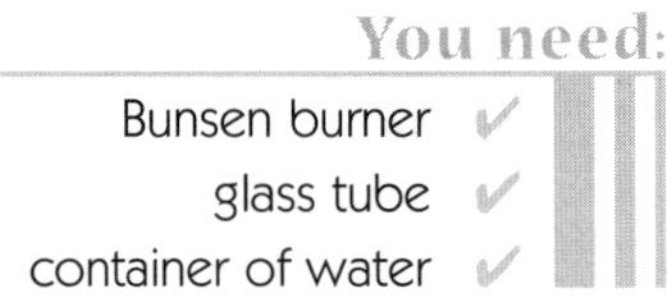


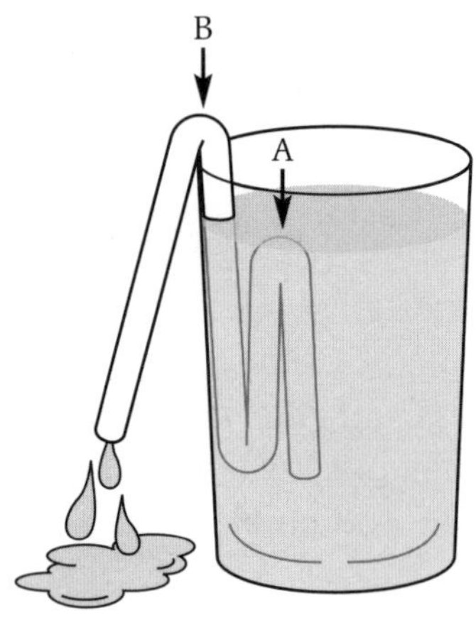


THERE ARE VARIOUS WAYS TO start a siphon working. Here's a curious siphon that starts itself!

Using a Bunsen burner to heat a glass tube, bend the tube into the shape shown. If you plunge it into a container of water, as soon as Bend A is below the water's level, the tube will become a siphon that will drain off all the water from the container!

This is the simplest of many different self-starting siphons that have been invented, some going back to ancient Greece.

## Why does it work?

When the water rushes through the tube to seek its own level, its inertia is sufficient to carry it above bend B and start the siphon working.

# 11

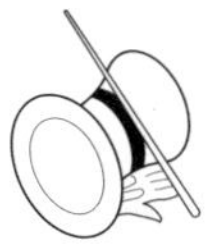

# A WATERMARK CODE

**You need:**

- 2 sheets of blank paper
- ballpoint pen

THIS IS SURELY ONE OF THE simplest ways to send a secret letter.

Wet a sheet of paper and spread it over a hard surface such as a smooth desk top, a mirror, or a glass window. Place a dry sheet of paper over the wet one and write a message on the dry paper by pressing hard with a ballpoint pen. Remove the papers from the desk top or glass. The message you wrote is clearly visible as a watermark on the wet sheet. When the sheet dries, the writing vanishes. It comes back again if the sheet is wet.

## Why does it work?

Pressure from the pen on the dry sheet of paper alters the fibers of the wet sheet beneath. This alteration is invisible when the sheet is dry, but becomes visible when it is wet again.

# 12

# MORE OR LESS THAN HALF FULL?

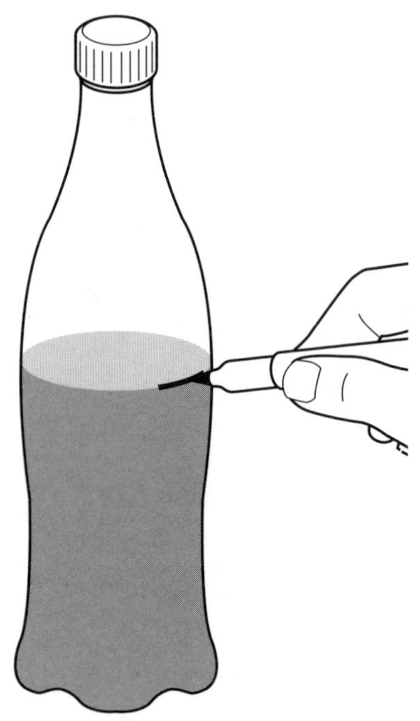

A CAPPED BOTTLE SEEMS TO be about half full of water. The bottle has a long neck, making it difficult to know for sure exactly whether the water fills more than half of the bottle's volume, less than half, or exactly half. Can you tell? How?

**Solution**: On the outside of the bottle, mark the level of water when the bottle is upright. Turn the bottle upside down. If the water level is now above the mark, the bottle is more than half full. If below the mark, less than half, and exactly half if it is right on the mark.

# 13

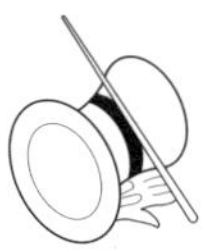

# SUSPENDED WATER

A WELL-KNOWN STUNT IS to place a sheet of paper over a glass that is half filled with water. With your palm on top of the paper, invert the glass. Carefully remove your hand. Air pressure keeps the water from spilling out by pressing the sheet tightly to the rim of the glass. At your command, the water falls out of the glass.

You need:

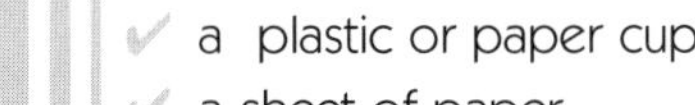

- a plastic or paper cup
- a sheet of paper
- a sharp pencil

## new!

Here's a new switch on this old trick.

Using a pencil, punch a hole near the bottom of a plastic or paper cup. Do the familiar trick (above) over a sink or outdoors. Keeping your thumb on the hole prevents air from entering above the water, and the paper will cling to the inverted glass, as expected.

Now announce that, on the count of three, you will cause the paper and water to drop. All you need do to make this happen is to slide your thumb off the hole!

### Why does it work?

As long as the hole in the glass is covered, it maintains a partial vacuum inside, and outside air pressure keeps the sheet pressed to the glass. When the hole is uncovered, it breaks the vacuum, allowing outside air pressure to enter the glass.

# 14

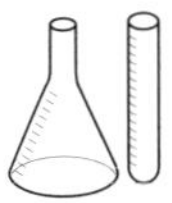

# A TABLE TENNIS BALL EXPERIMENT

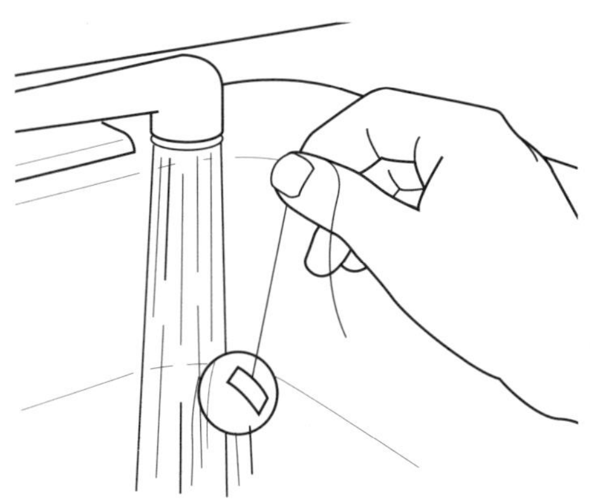

A TABLE TENNIS BALL CURIOUSLY REFUSES TO LEAVE A STREAM of water.

Attach one end of the thread to the Ping-Pong ball with a piece of tape. Turn on a sink faucet and push the ball halfway into the stream as shown. You would expect the force of the water to knock the ball out of the stream, but it doesn't! The ball remains fixed inside the stream!

**You need:**

- a foot-long (30cm) thread
- Ping-Pong ball
- tape
- faucet

## Why does it work?

The water, flowing rapidly over half the ball's surface, reduces the air pressure on that side of the ball. The higher air pressure on the ball's other side keeps forcing the ball back into the stream of water.

# 15

# A TWO-COLORED FLOWER

**You need:**

- a white flower, such as a rose or carnation
- scissors (optional)
- 2 glasses of water
- food coloring, red and blue

YOU'VE PROBABLY NEVER seen a flower that was half red and half blue, but it's easy to make one.

Take the white flower, and, with scissors or your fingernail, split the flower's stem in half. Trim off the ends of each half-stem.

Fill two glasses with water. In one of them pour in some blue food coloring until the water is dark blue. In the other glass pour in red coloring. Put one of the half stems in each glass, as shown in the picture. In a few hours, one half of the white flower will turn blue and the other half red!

## Why does it work?

The flower's stem consists of many tiny tubes, half of which go to one side of the blossom and half to the other side. Capillary attraction draws the colored water upward into each half of the blossom to bi-color it.

# 16

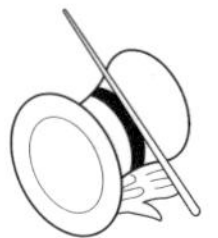

# AN ICE CUBE LIFTER

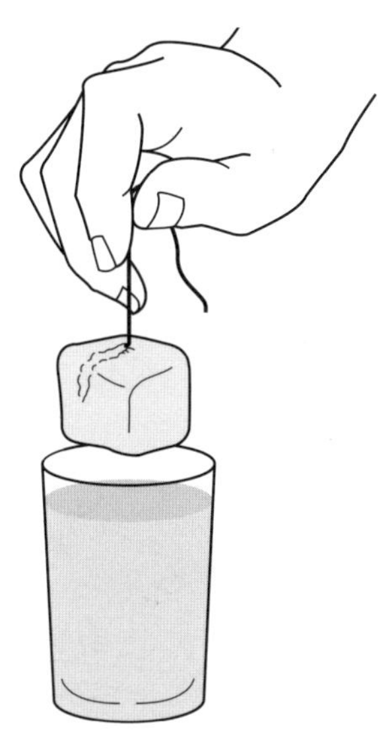

AN ICE CUBE FLOATS IN A GLASS OF water. Beside it is a piece of string. Tell your friends that you can use the string to lift the cube out of the glass.

It seems impossible. Here's what you do. Lay one end of the string across the top of the cube. Sprinkle a good amount of salt on the string. Lift the string and the cube will come with it!

## Why does it work?

**You need:**

- ✓ ice cube
- ✓ glass of water
- ✓ string
- ✓ salt

Ice cubes in water are continually shrinking and growing because their surfaces melt and then re-freeze. When you add salt to the ice cube, it keeps the water from re-freezing at the surface of the cube. Salt does this by getting in the way of the water molecules that are trying to re-form into ice. But since the cube is surrounded by water, the salt eventually gets carried away into the rest of the glass. With less salt, the water molecules can once again become ice. Only now, the new ice freezes around the string and holds it in place so you can lift the cube.

# 17

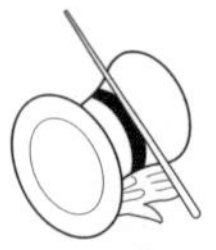

# A FLOATING COIN

**You need:**

- a 1-yen coin (Japanese currency)
- Bowl filled with water
- paper clip
- liquid detergent

THE 1-YEN COINS USED IN JAPAN ARE MADE OF ALUMINUM so light in weight that they can be made to float on water.

Fill a bowl with water. When the water is still, balance a yen on a paper clip and carefully lower the yen to the water's surface. It will float.

Now let a drop of liquid detergent fall on the water. The yen will sink instantly.

Why?

## Why does it work?

The surface of water has the ability to support objects that normally would sink. This is called the water's "surface tension." It works because water molecules attract each other.

All the molecules pull on each other, but those on the surface are only pulled by molecules beneath them. So these molecules are held very tightly together and keep other objects from penetrating the water's surface. For an object to stay on the surface it must be fairly light and composed of molecules that repel the water molecules. Such molecules are called "hydrophobic." Aluminum and most metals are hydrophobic.

When you put a drop of liquid detergent in the water, it greatly reduces the water's surface tension. The detergent molecules have one end that is hydrophobic, or repulsed by water, while the other end is "hydrophilic," or attracted to water. They form a thin film on the water's surface with their hydrophilic ends pointing in and their hydrophobic ends pointing out. They aren't strongly attracted to one another and they get in the way of water molecules at the surface as well. Overall, the surface tension is greatly reduced and the yen will sink.

# II. motion, inertia, friction

# 18

# THE TWIRLED RING

As all physicists know, when an ice skater spins with outstretched arms, then quickly lowers her arms, her rotation speed increases enormously. It is the result, of course, of her arms suddenly being forced to move in a smaller circular path.

This effect can be neatly demonstrated with a finger ring and piece of string. Put the ring on the string, allowing it to hang down, as shown, while you hold the ends of the string.

Twirl the ring in a circle about six inches (15cm) in diameter. While you are twirling the ring, pull on the ends of the string. The ring will speed up.

**You need:**

- a ring
- a string

## Why does it work?

When you pull on the ends of the string, the ring is forced to revolve in a much smaller orbit, causing its angular velocity to suddenly increase.

The same thing happens when water goes down the drain of a sink. Give the water a circular motion with your hand. As the spiralling water diminishes in area, it spins in smaller and smaller circles and with increasing speed.

# 19

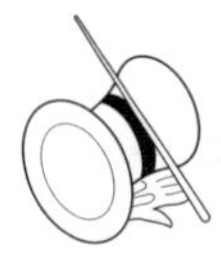

# A NEWSPAPER TRICK

**You need:**

a sheet of newspaper

HOLD A SHEET OF newspaper in your left hand, letting the sheet hang down as shown. Can you poke your index finger through the paper?

It may seem unlikely, yet it is easy to do. Simply jab your finger as rapidly as you can at the center of the paper. If you do it fast enough, your finger will go right through!

### Why does it work?

Air pressure on the paper's far side keeps it rigid. This rigidity is further strengthened by the paper's inertia—the tendency of a body to resist being moved by an outside force.

# 20

# THE UNBROKEN TISSUE

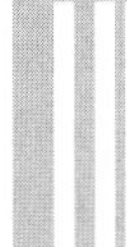

**You need:**

- a cardboard tube
- a rubber band
- a piece of tissue paper
- grains of uncooked rice

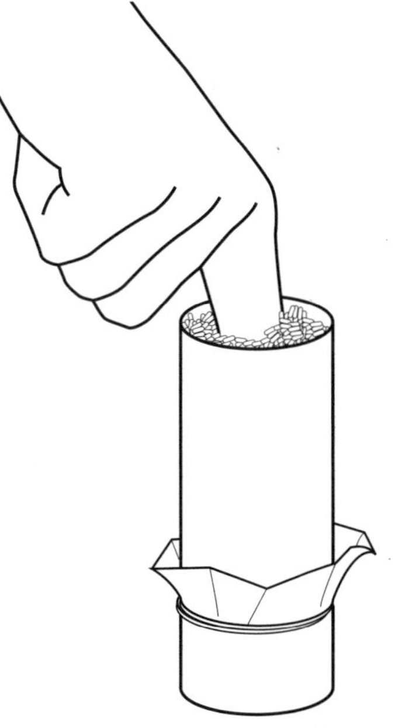

WHY DOESN'T THE TISSUE paper break?

Using a rubber band, attach a square of tissue paper across one end of a cardboard tube, such as the one that comes inside a toilet paper roll. Hold the tube vertically, open end up, and fill the tube with uncooked rice. You'd think that by pressing down as hard as you can with your thumb on top of the rice, you could break the tissue paper at the other end of the tube.

Well, you can't!

Why?

## Why does it work?

The grains of rice are hard and slippery and they can easily slip around each other. So the pressure you apply to one end of the tube is evenly distributed among all the rice grains. Some of the pressure goes into the cardboard tube, which can withstand it without breaking. There is also pressure on the tissue, but it is distributed across the tissue's surface, making it less likely to break at any one spot. This is a good model for the air pressure in a balloon or tire. The air molecules also slip around and bounce against each other easily, so the pressure is evenly distributed throughout the balloon or tire.

# 21

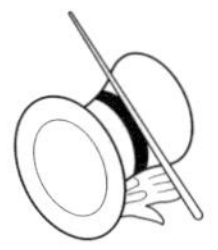

# CRAZY BOUNCE

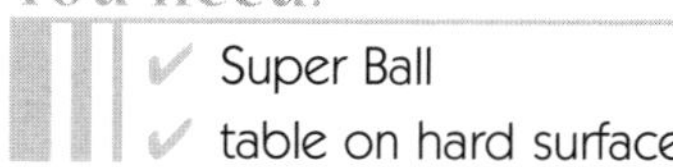


SUPER BALLS—BOUNCING BALLS made of hard rubber—are sold in many toy stores. The slightest spin on such a ball causes it to bounce in a crazy way.

For example, try this on a table that is standing on a hard surface. Throw the ball as shown by the zigzag arrow. It will hit the table's underside, reverse direction, and bounce back to you!

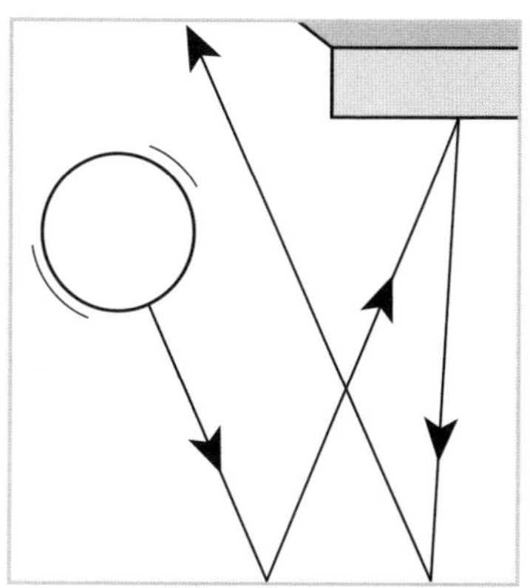

### Why does it work?

When the Super Ball hits the underside of the table at a slant, it puts a strong backspin on the ball. This causes the ball to bounce backward.

Here's something to amuse your friends. Tell them you have discovered a technique by which you can throw the ball in such a way that it will stop in midair, reverse direction, and come back to you. Your friends will want to see that!

How do you do it? Just toss the ball straight up in the air. Follow this by saying you are also able to drop the ball from a height of four feet, and it will not hit the floor. How? Drop it and catch it with your other hand.

# 22

# CATCH THE DICE

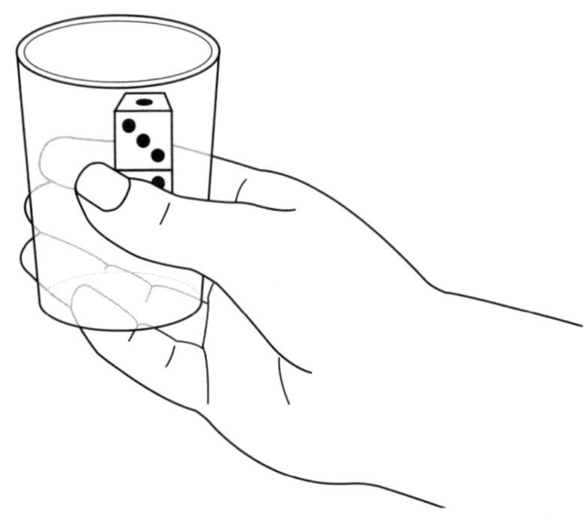

THIS IS A "BETCHA" THAT YOU CAN TRY ON YOUR friends.

With your thumb, hold two dice against the side of a glass, as shown. The tricky task is to toss the dice in the air, one at a time, and catch each in the glass. The top die is easy to toss and catch. But when you try to do the same thing with the other die, the first one flies out of the glass. Let your friends try to do it. They won't be able to either. How can you catch them both?

**You need:**

- 2 dice ✓
- glass ✓

**Solution:** The secret is to not throw the second die. Just let it go and quickly lower the glass to catch it. Although the first die may hop upward a short distance, inertia will keep it from falling faster than the glass is moving down, and it will stay inside the glass.

# 23

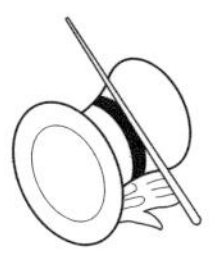

# THE SUSPENDED BOTTLE

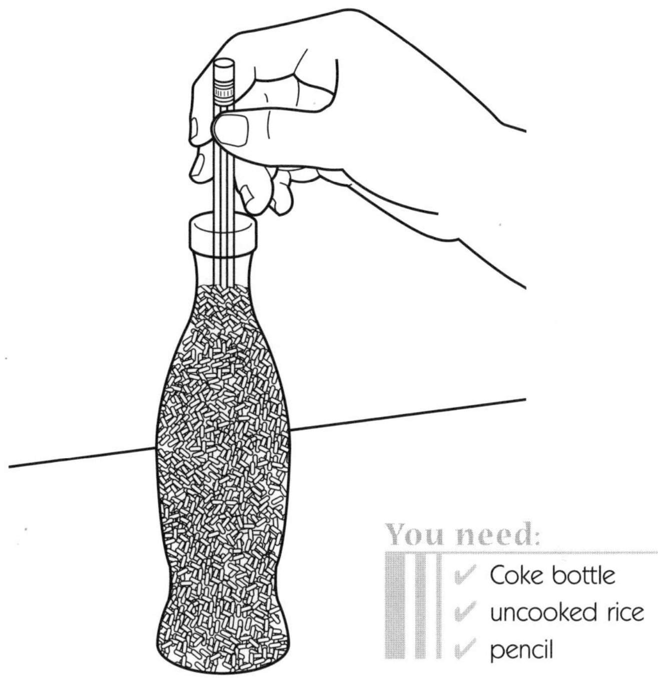

**You need:**

- Coke bottle
- uncooked rice
- pencil

FILL A COKE BOTTLE WITH UNCOOKED RICE. PLUNGE A PENCIL, a chopstick, or any similar rod straight down into the rice, and you'll find that when you lift the pencil, the bottle goes with it! You may have to plunge the pencil into the bottle more than once before it sticks.

Then give the pencil a twist and you'll be able to remove it from the rice easily.

This works with any bottle or bowl as long as its opening has a smaller circumference than the bottle. The trick comes from India, where fakirs (magicians) plunge a dagger into a large bowl of rice, and then lift the dagger to display a bowl miraculously suspended on the dagger's blade.

### Why does it work?

The explanation is similar to that of the unbroken tissue (see page 36). The force introduced by the pencil is distributed among the tightly packed rice grains. They are forced to press firmly both against the pencil and the sides of the bottle. Twisting the pencil breaks these forces, and allows the pencil to be removed easily.

# 24

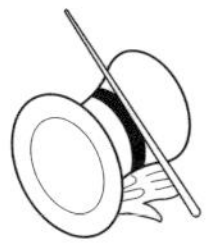

# SHUFFLED PAGES

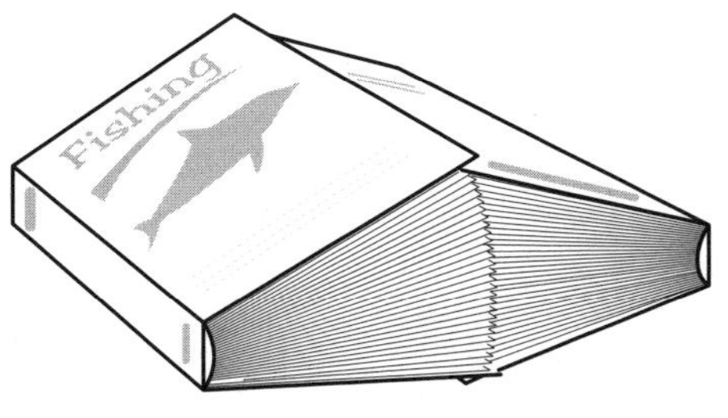


THIS TRICK SEEMS TO turn books into very strong magnets.

Take the two books—they can be either hardcover or paperback—and place them on a table with their front edges touching. Treat the books as if they are the two halves of a deck of cards that you will shuffle together. Let the pages fall slowly from your thumbs, allowing them to thoroughly interlace. After the shuffle, force the books as close together as you can.

Challenge someone to grasp the spines of the books and pull the books apart. It can't be done!

**You need:**

- 2 books of the same size and number of pages
- table

## Why does it work?

A slight amount of friction develops between any two pages that are from opposite books. The effect is magnified by the many coupled pages into a strong friction that keeps the books from separating.

# 25

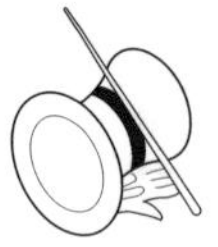

# THREE DROP TASKS

You need:

a matchbox ✔

a paper match ✔

a cylindrical cork ✔

**1** FROM A HEIGHT OF SIX INCHES (15CM) ABOVE A TABLETOP, drop a matchbox so that it lands on its end and remains upright.

**2** Drop a paper match so it lands and stays on its edge.

**3** Drop a cylindrical cork so that it lands on one end.

All three of these feats are impossible, unless you know something sneaky.

For 1: Secretly push the matchbox drawer about an inch upward as you hold the box vertically. You can conceal the projection with your hand. The matchbox won't bounce.

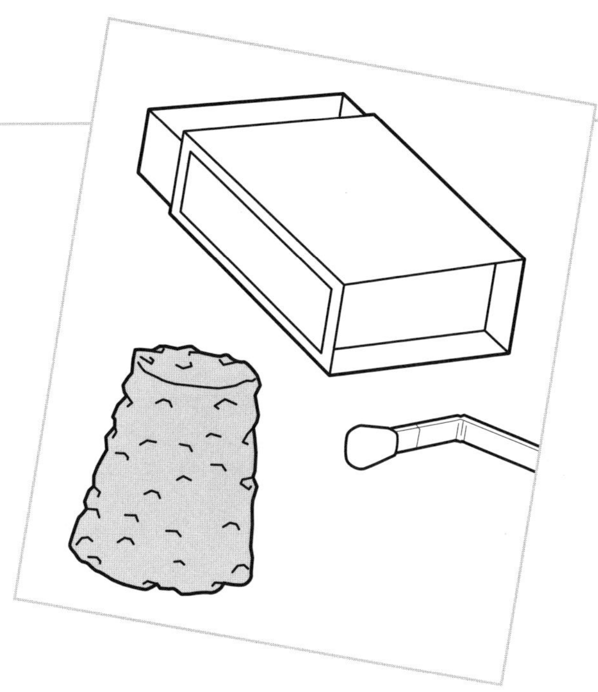

For 2: Bend the match in the middle before you drop it.

For 3: Drop the cork on its side, and after a few failures it will bounce up and land balanced on its end.

## Why does it work?

For 1: When the box hits the table, the inertia of the drawer sliding back into place uses up the energy that would have gone into a bounce.

For 2: A straight match is unlikely to stand on its edge, but bending it forces it to land on its edge.

For 3: If the cork lands on either end, it tends to bounce to land on its side. But when dropped on its side, it frequently will bounce to land on one of its ends.

# 26

# TWIDDLED BOLTS

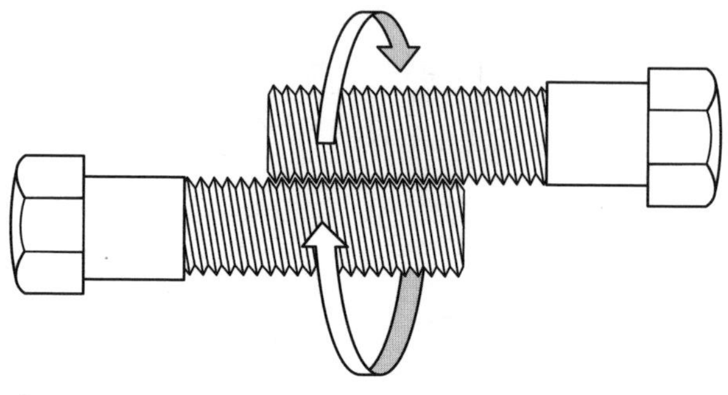

HERE IS A PUZZLE TO DO IN YOUR HEAD. IMAGINE THAT TWO identical bolts are placed together so that their three-dimensional spiral structures, called a helix, intermesh, as in the picture below.

Now, in your mind, move the bolts around each other, as if you were twiddling your thumbs, holding each bolt firmly by the head so that it doesn't rotate. Twiddle the bolts in the direction shown by the arrow. Do you think the heads will

a. move inward
b. move outward
c. remain the same distance from each other?

**Solution**: Most people are surprised to learn that the answer is c. It is comparable to someone walking up an escalator that is moving downward.

# 27

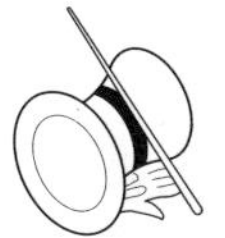

# THE RISING COIN

HOLD AN EMPTY MATCHBOX VERTICALLY AND INSERT A COIN between the cover and the underside of the drawer, as shown below.

Grasp the box in your left hand. With a pencil or pen, tap the top end of the box. The pen must simultaneously hit the two corners indicated by arrows.

**You need:**

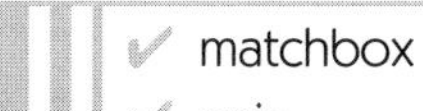

- matchbox
- coin
- pencil or pen

As you continue tapping, the coin will rise slowly through the box until it emerges at the top.

Thanks to Tan Bah Chee, a Singapore magician, who published this stunt in a magic magazine in 1974.

### Why does it work?

Each tap of the matchbox lowers it a trifle, but the coin's inertia causes it to stay at its same height. Thus, with each tap, the coin rises a trifle between the box and its cover, until it reaches the top of the box.

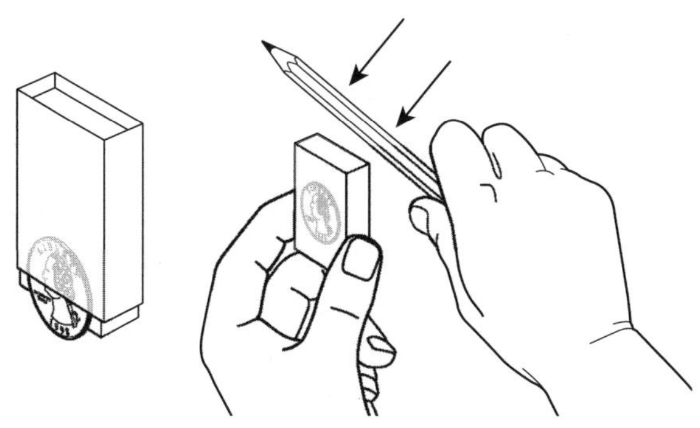

# 28

# A YARDSTICK QUESTION

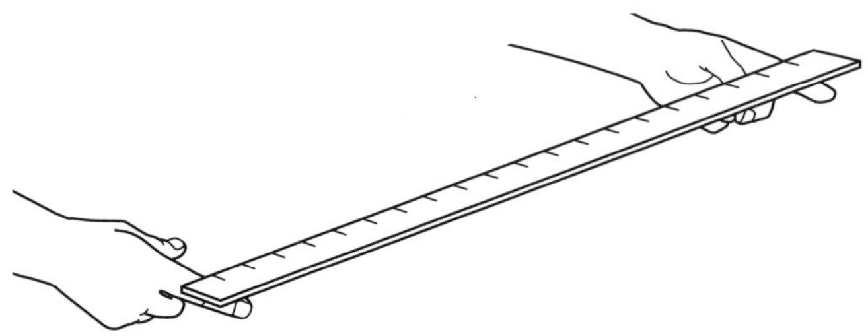

IT IS NOW WELL KNOWN THAT IF YOU REST A YARDSTICK ON YOUR extended forefingers, one at each end, and then move them toward each other, they will always meet at the center of the yardstick. This isn't hard to explain. If one finger gets ahead of the other, weight on that finger increases. This increases the friction between the stick and the finger, and lowers friction on the other finger, allowing it to move ahead.

You need:
a yardstick

**Now for the question:** With both fingers at the center of the yardstick, what happens if you try to move them back to the ends of the stick where they started? Try guessing the answer before you try it. You may be surprised.

**Answer:** As soon as one finger starts to move, its friction against the yardstick decreases. The farther it moves, the less the friction. The result is that the first finger to move will go all the way to the end, while the other finger will remain at the stick's center.

# 29

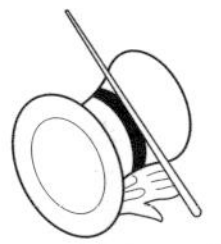

# TWO ROLLERS AND A YARDSTICK

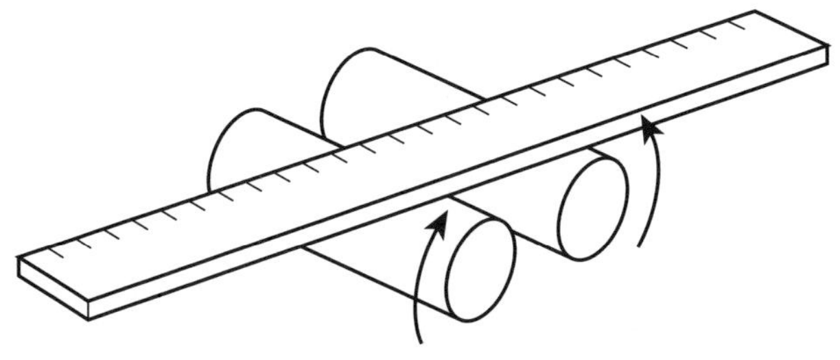

PLACE TWO PAPER-TOWEL OR TOILET-TISSUE TUBES SIDE BY side, and balance a yardstick on top of them, as shown.

If you rotate the tubes inward, in opposite directions as indicated by the arrows, the yardstick remains balanced on the tubes. It may shift back and forth slightly, but it remains balanced. Now try rotating the tubes the opposite way. The stick will slowly travel to one side until it falls off the tubes!

## Why does it work?

**You need:**

- 2 cardboard tubes (from paper towel or toilet tissue)
- yardstick

The action results from a merger of weight and friction.

Consider the case when the tubes rotate inward. The instant the stick shifts slightly to one side—say the left—its weight on the leftmost tube increases. This naturally increases friction between tube and stick. With more friction on the left tube than on the right, the rotating left tube moves the stick back into balance.

# 30

# ROTATING CYLINDERS

You need:

- 2 toilet tissue tubes
- large cylindrical can

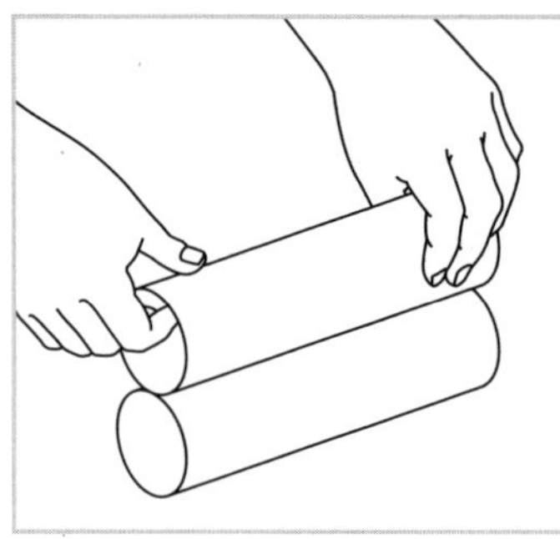

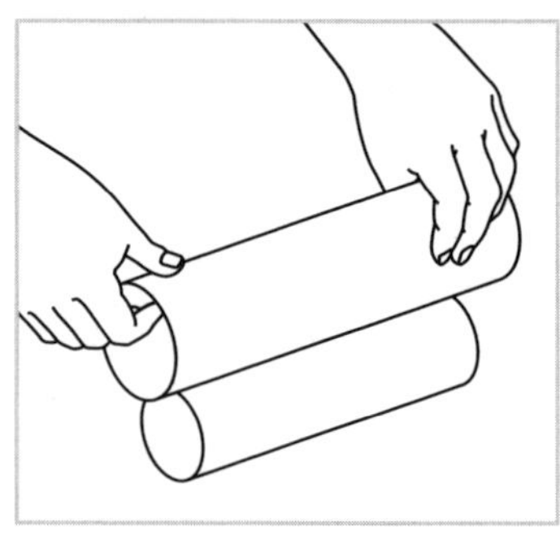

PLACE ONE TOILET PAPER TUBE on top of another, as shown in the top figure. Move them across the table by rotating the top tube with your fingers. As you would guess, the bottom tube rotates the opposite way, and the two tubes travel together.

Now replace the top tube with a large cylindrical can, as shown in the bottom figure. If you rotate the can, will the cardboard tube travel smoothly along with the can as before, or will it slip free of the can by moving faster or slower than the can?

It may surprise you that the two travel together as if they were the same size.

## Why does it work?

The point of contact between the two objects travels with the same speed and distance on each object. This is independent of the relative sizes of the two rolling objects.

31

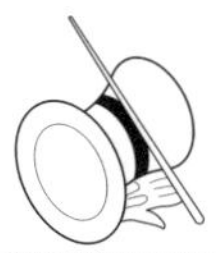

# A NOVEL WAY TO FIND A SELECTED CARD

THERE ARE HUNDREDS OF WAYS a magician can find a selected card. This is one of the most mysterious.

Someone selects a card from the deck, notes what it is, and then cuts the deck in half, inserting the card between the two halves. You pick up the deck and toss it on the table. The deck mysteriously breaks in two, with the top half sliding off the bottom portion. The bottom card of the top half proves to be the selected card!

**You need:**

- a deck of cards
- salt

**The Secret:** You have a bit of salt in a side pocket. While the card is being chosen, moisten the tip of your index finger and touch it to the salt to pick up some grains. After the deck is cut in half, tap your finger on either half as you say, "Place your card here." A few grains of salt will fall invisibly on top of the half. Put the other half on the salted one.

Toss the restored deck on the table with a forward motion. The salt grains cause the top half to slide over the bottom half. Show that the bottom card of the top half is the chosen card.

# 32

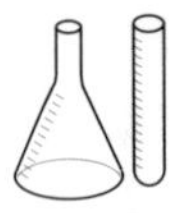

# TWO WAYS TO BREAK A PENCIL

**You need:**

- 3 sheets of newspaper
- table
- 2 new pencils
- dollar bill

1 PLACE THREE SHEETS OF NEWSPAPER ON THE SIDE OF A TABLE with a new pencil halfway under the paper. Let the other half of the pencil project over the edge of the table, as shown in the picture. Strike the end of the pencil with a quick blow of your hand, or hit it with a hammer. The newspaper will not tear, but the pencil will break in half! In similar fashion, you can break a ruler, a shingle, or any thin wooden board.

2 Crease a dollar bill lengthwise, making the crease as sharp as possible. Explain that it will act like the edge of a knife and chop a pencil in half. Have someone hold the pencil horizontally by grasping the two ends. Hit the center of the pencil once or twice with the folded edge of the bill. Nothing happens. On the next attempt the pencil is sliced neatly in half.

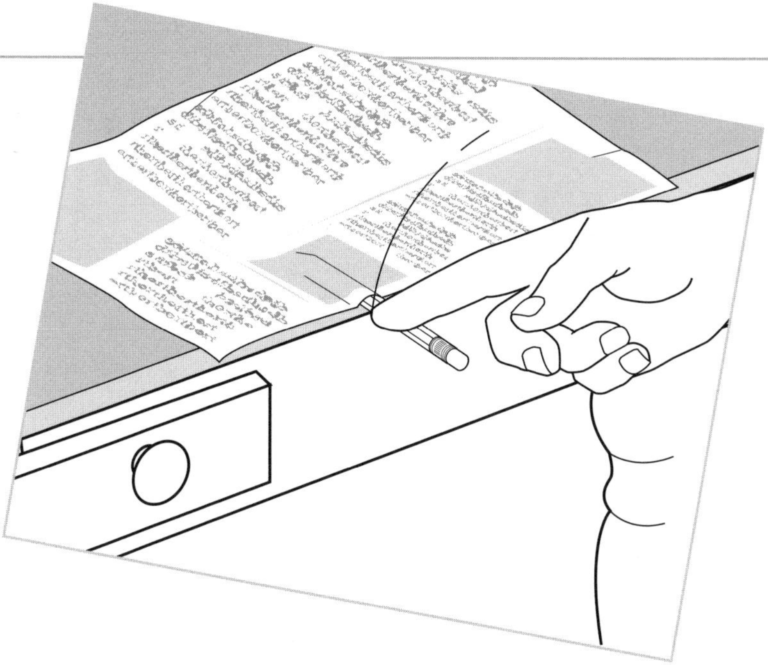

## The Secret:

As you hit the pencil, secretly extend your forefinger alongside the bill. The momentum of your finger will snap the pencil in half without damaging your finger in the least.

## Why does it work?

Inertia and air pressure keep the newspaper intact, allowing the pencil to break. And it is the inertia of your finger that breaks the pencil when someone is holding its ends.

# 33

# A FOUR-LEGGED LEMON BUG

You need:

- a paper napkin or paper towel
- felt-tip pen
- a lemon

IT'S EASY TO MAKE A PAPER BUG. ITS WOBBLY MOTION ACROSS the floor makes most people think there is a complicated mechanism inside.

Children and even some adults will be amused by this stunt. The bug is made by twisting the corners of a paper napkin or paper towel to make the bug's four legs, as shown. Add eyes to the bug with a felt tip pen.

When you push on the back of the bug, it glides over the table or a hardwood floor with a very funny wobbly motion. What's causing the bug's weird motion? No one will be able to guess.

**The Secret:** Lift the bug and reveal a lemon that you have secretly placed under the napkin.

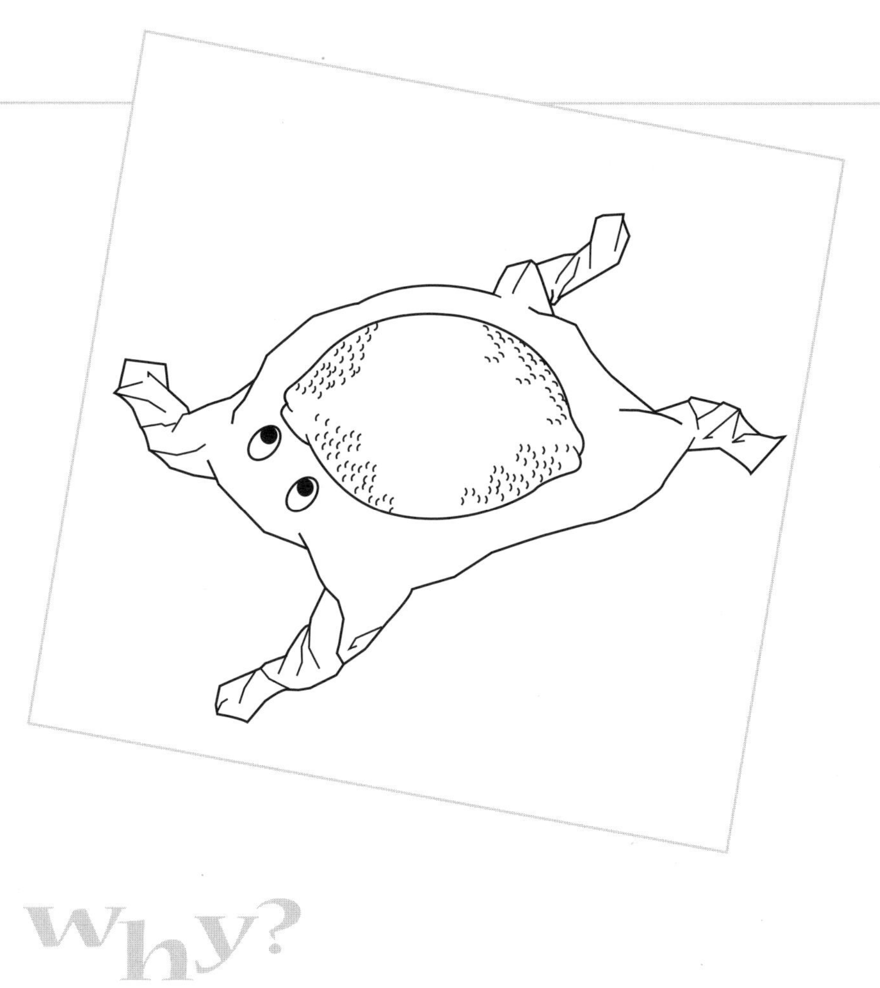

Why?

## Why does it work?

The lemon has rounded ends so it rolls easily, but its irregular shape causes it to roll with a funny, wobbling motion. This makes the Lemon Bug look like a real insect when it moves, because some insects, and other small creatures, will often move in an erratic way to elude predators—or people who want to step on them.

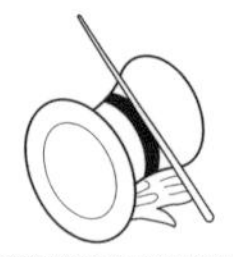

# 34

# THE WALKING HAIRPIN

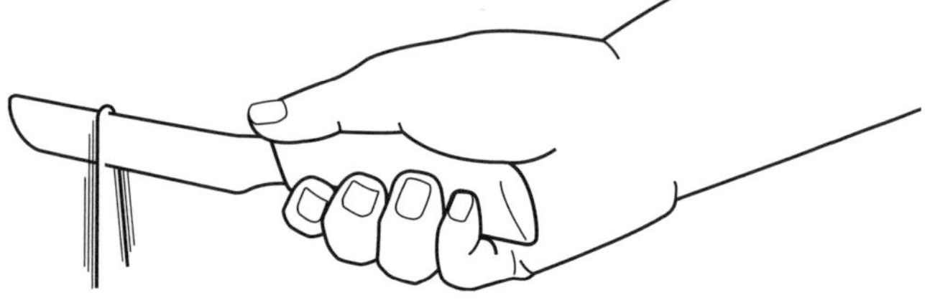

**You need:**

- a hairpin, paper clip, or toothpick
- a table knife

A HAIRPIN MOVES ALONG THE EDGE OF A table knife.

Place a hairpin over the edge of a table knife and hold the knife horizontally, with the hairpin leaning toward you as shown. No matter how hard you try to keep the knife steady (your arm must not be resting on the table), you'll find the hairpin "walking" toward your hand. Push the hairpin so that it leans the other way and it will walk forward until it falls off the knife.

If you can't locate a hairpin, straighten a paper clip and bend it in the middle, or bend a toothpick without breaking it apart.

## Why does it work?

It is almost impossible to keep your hand from jiggling. Each jiggle lifts the pin a trifle. Because the hairpin is slanting, it comes to rest at a spot farther along the knife blade. Lean the hairpin the other way and it will crawl in the other direction.

# 35

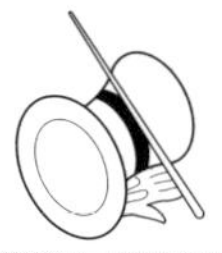

# THE "MAGNETIC" PEN

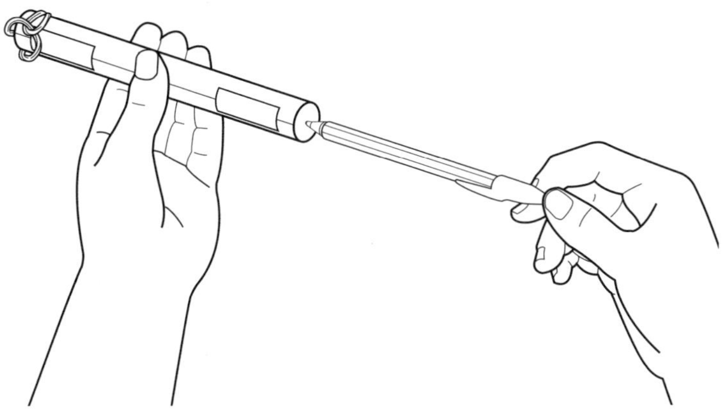

A PEN JUMPS MYSTERIOUSLY back into a tube, as if pulled by a magnet or a rubber band. But only you can make it work.

**You need:**

- a pencil
- a square of paper 6 x 6" (15 x 15cm)
- tape
- rubber band
- ballpoint pen with cap (as shown)

Roll a square of paper around a pencil to form a tube about six inches (15cm) long. A piece of tape will keep it from unrolling. Tape the end of a rubber band to one end of the empty tube, as shown, then push the rubber band into the tube.

You need a ballpoint pen with a cap shaped like the

one in the illustration. Insert the pen (point first) into the tube and pretend that you are trying to catch its pointed end on the rubber band. Pull the pen part way out of the tube. It snaps back into the tube as if it were jerked by the rubber band.

**The Secret:**

What actually happens is this: Your fingers squeeze the pointed cap the way you squeeze a watermelon seed to make it jump through the air. The illusion that something is pulling on the pen is so strong that when you hand the pen to the victim, he or she will try repeatedly to make the pen hop back into the tube—without success.

# 36

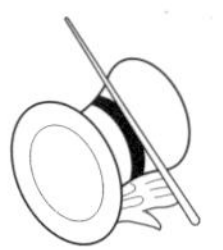

# THE SPOOL THAT ROLLS BACKWARD

**You need:**

- 2 cardboard disks about 3" (7.5cm) in diameter
- an empty wooden spool
- string

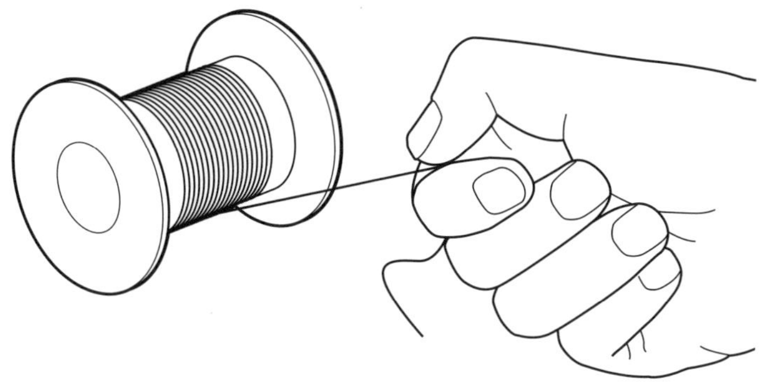

CUT THE TWO DISKS FROM CARDBOARD, AND GLUE THEM TO the ends of an empty wooden spool. Wrap a length of string around the spool. If you pull on the free end, as shown, will the large spool roll away from you? Toward you? Or will it stand still?

**Answer**: The spool will roll toward you.

## Why does it work?

A tug on the string seems as if it will make the spool roll away from you, but this is impossible because you are actually tugging it toward you. The larger disks on either side offer no such resistance to the pull. Consequently, the spool rolls toward you, while the string winds more and more around the spool.

The same phenomenon can be seen with a bicycle. Have someone steady the bike and move it until one pedal is directly below the other. Attach a rope to the bottom pedal. If you stand behind the bicycle and pull on the rope, it will try to turn the pedals in a direction that propels the bike forward. However, the bicycle actually will roll backward, for the same reason the spool does.

# 37

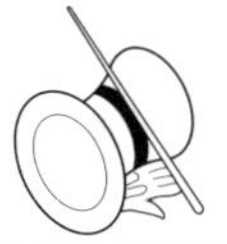

# A CARNIVAL SWINDLE

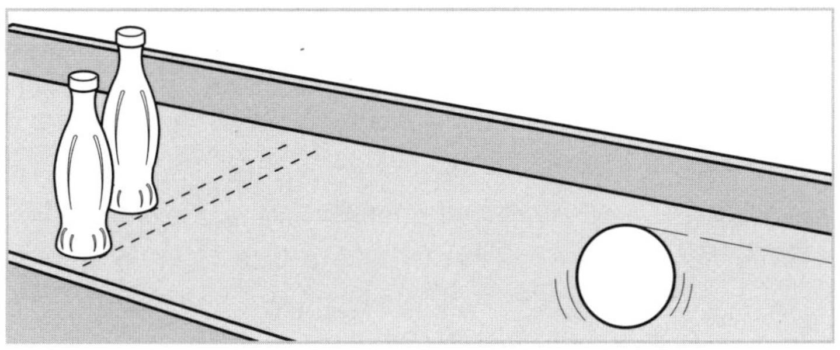

A CARNIVAL GAME IS CALLED A TWO-WAY STORE WHEN IT IS "gaffed" so the operator can demonstrate how easy it is to win, yet when a player tries, he invariably loses. Here's an example of such a game.

Place two empty Coke bottles side by side as shown, and roll a ball (such as a baseball, croquet ball, or billiard ball) toward them. Both fall over. When anyone else tries to knock down the two bottles, only one falls over.

**You need:**

- 2 Coke bottles
- a ball

**The Secret:** Here is the gaff. When you set the bottles for the "mark" (carnival slang for "sucker"), place one bottle about an eighth of an inch behind the other. From the front, the difference is not noticeable. The ball now is sure to hit one bottle first, and then rebound, leaving the other bottle standing.

# 38

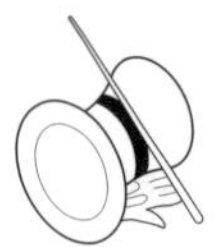

# THE MYSTERIOUS WHIMMY DIDDLE

You need:

- 2 pencils
- a file
- a pin
- a rectangular piece of cardboard

IN THE APPALACHIAN MOUNTAINS, where this toy dates back hundreds of years, it is called a Whimmy Diddle. Thousands of wooden versions are sold each year, and a Gee Haw Whimmy Diddle Competition is held every summer at Asheville's Folk Art Center. "Gee" is the propeller's spin to the right, and "haw" is its spin to the left. The Whimmy Diddle is easy to make.

Cut notches along the edge of a pencil. Stick a pin through the center of the cardboard and attach it to the pencil's eraser, as shown in the top figure. The hole in the "propeller" must be a bit larger than the pin, in order to cut down friction.

Hold the end of the pencil in your left hand. With your right hand, rub the second pencil back and forth across the notches as shown. If the tip of your first finger slides along the right side of the notches, the cardboard propeller will rotate rapidly in the "gee" direction. If you move the rubbing pencil a trifle forward so that the tip of your thumb now slides along the left side of the notches, the propeller will stop and whirl the "haw" way!

The movement of your right hand is undetectable. This allows you to command the propeller to rotate first one way, and then the other, without revealing how you do it.

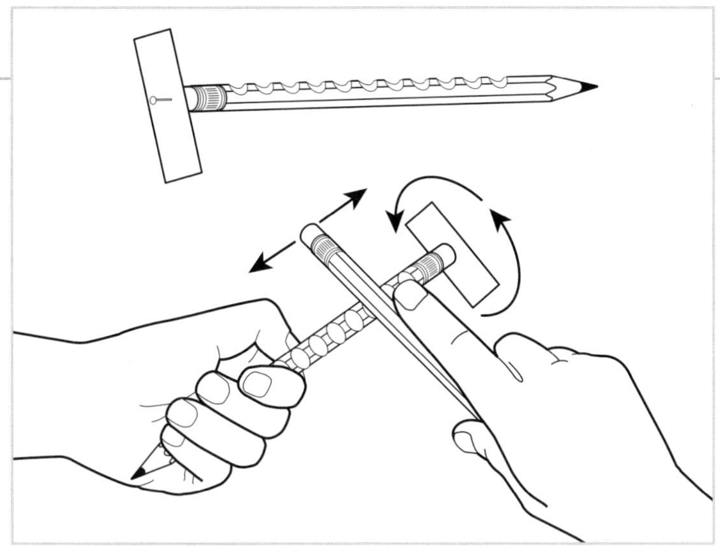

## Why does it work?

The spin of the propeller is caused by horizontal—or back and forth—vibrations in the notched pencil as you run the second pencil over it. These horizontal vibrations have a specific oscillation pattern that creates vertical—or up and down—vibrations in the pin. The pin's vertical vibrations take the form of circular or elliptical motion, and this motion causes the propeller to spin.

When you hold a finger against the left side of the notched pencil, you force the horizontal vibrations to travel in one direction and create vertical vibrations in the same direction. This causes the propeller to spin "gee," or left. When you hold a finger against the right side of notched pencil, the vibrations travel in the opposite direction and cause the propeller to spin "haw," or right.

# 39

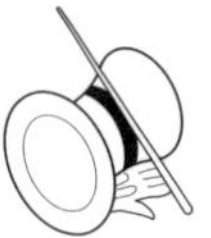

# THE LINKING PAPER CLIPS

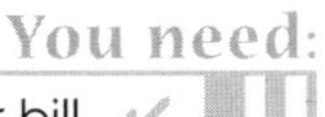


- a dollar bill
- 2 paper clips
- 2 thin rubber bands

ALMOST EVERYONE KNOWS THE TRICK WITH A DOLLAR BILL folded as shown, with two paper clips added. When you pull apart the ends of the bill, until the bill is flat, the two clips jump off the bill linked. Here is a little-known elaboration by Nob Yoshigahara of Tokyo.

Put two thin elastic bands around the bill, just inside each fold, as shown. Now pull the bill flat—and be surprised by what happens! The result is a chain, with two clips in the middle and a rubber band at each end.

## Why does it work?

Pull very slowly on the ends of the bill and you'll see how it works. The positions of the clips and rubber bands are such that they are forced to interlink to form the chain.

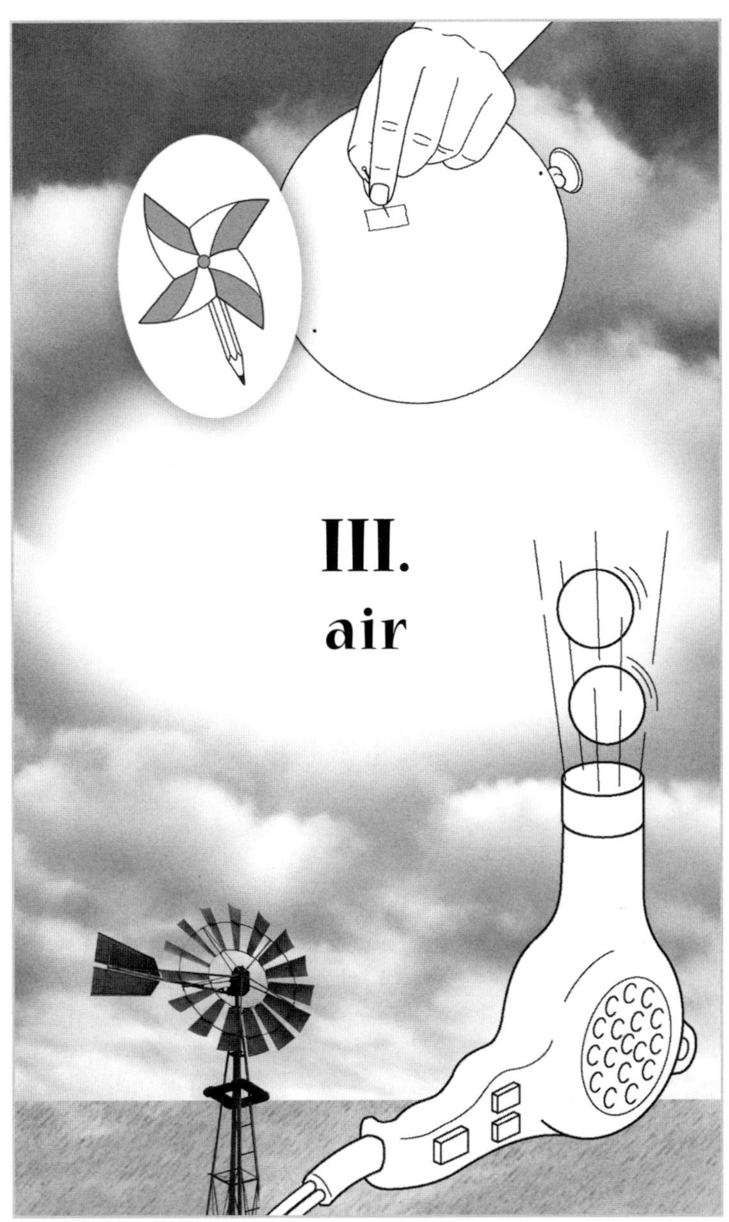

# III. air

# 40

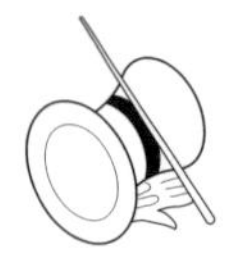

# THE JUMPING PENCIL

USING A LARGE NAIL, PUNCH A HOLE NEAR THE BOTTOM OF AN empty, hard plastic bottle. Lower a balloon into the bottle and spread its mouth over the bottle's mouth, as shown. Inflate the balloon by blowing into it. Then put your thumb over the hole in the bottle. Your friends, unaware of the hole, will be puzzled by the fact that the balloon remains inflated.

**You need:**

- large nail
- plastic bottle
- balloon
- pencil or swizzle stick

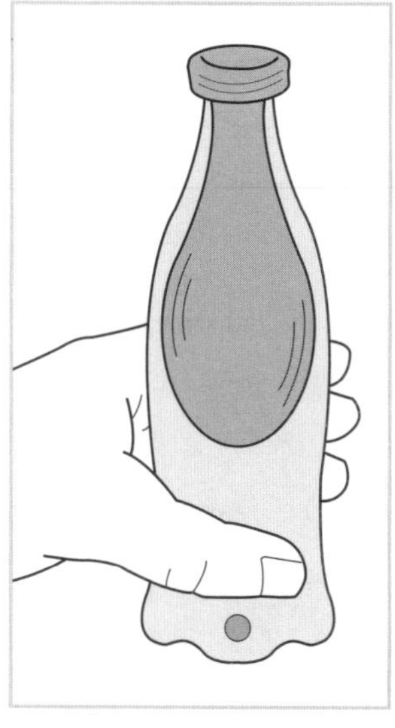

Drop a pencil or swizzle stick into the balloon. Count to three. On the last count, remove your thumb from the hole. The balloon will deflate quickly, sending the pencil high into the air.

### Why does it work?

When the balloon is inflated in the bottle and your finger covers the hole, this creates a partial vacuum that keeps outside air from rushing in. When the hole is uncovered, the vacuum is destroyed, and the balloon deflates so rapidly that it shoots out the pencil.

# 41

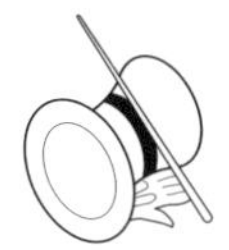

# A CARD DROP CHALLENGE

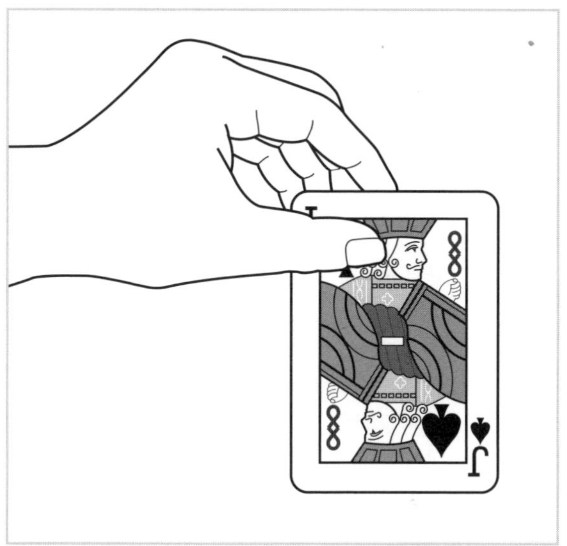

You need:

- a magazine
- playing cards

PLACE A MAGAZINE FLAT ON THE FLOOR. Hand six playing cards to a friend and ask her to drop each card from a height of a few feet, so it lands on the magazine. As you say this, hold a card vertically, as shown, but without saying that the card must be held that way before it is dropped.

If she holds the card this way before dropping it, it will flutter to one side, missing the magazine.

Now you show the only way to do it. Hold the card

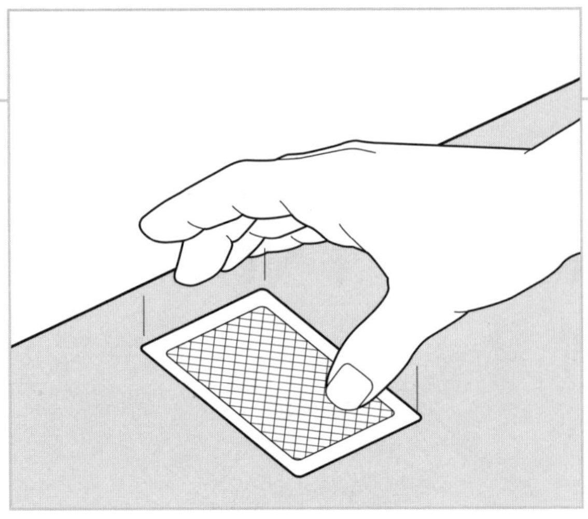

horizontally by a thumb at one end and your fingers at the other end, so the card is parallel to the floor. Let go. The card will fall on the magazine.

## Why does it work?

When you drop a card, gravity pulls it toward the floor, but the surrounding air resists its downward motion. If you drop the card horizontally, the air resistance is equal over the surface of the card, so it floats straight down toward the magazine. If you drop the card vertically, the thin edge of the card cuts through the air quickly, but the larger, flat surfaces are likely to encounter turbulence and small air currents that cause the card to turn slightly. As it turns, the card begins to slip sideways through the air, following its thin leading edge that has less air resistance. The slipping card misses the magazine.

# 42

# SHOOT A PLAYING CARD

**You need:**

- 1 jack from an old deck of cards

YOUR FINGER HAS FIRING power.

Pick one of the jacks in an old deck of cards to be the bad guy. Bend the card and stand it on the table as shown.

You are the good guy. Pointing your finger to the left, swing your hand suddenly clockwise, until you are pointing directly at the jack, shout "POW!" and the jack falls over!

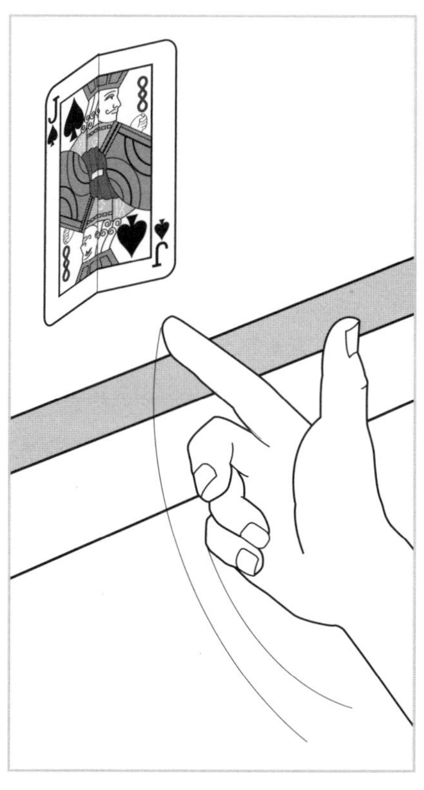

## Why does it work?

The breeze created by your hand, which can be more than a foot away from the card, does the job.

# 43

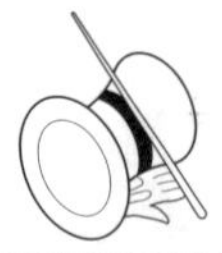

# THE SODA STRAW "BETCHA"

You need:

2 straws ✓
a glass of water ✓

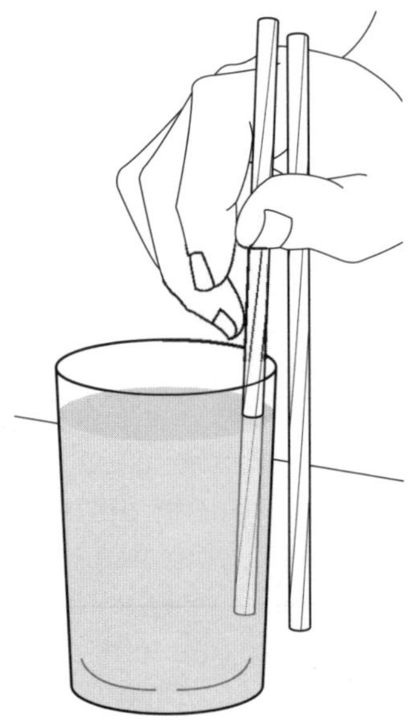

PUT ONE STRAW INTO A glass of water. Beside it, but outside the glass, put another straw. Challenge one of your friends to put the ends of the two straws in his or her mouth and drink some water.

It can't be done!

But you can do it easily.

**The Secret**: Put your tongue over the end of the outside straw.

### Why does it work?

When the outside straw is open at both ends, you can only suck air through this straw. When the top of this straw is closed by your tongue, you can draw liquid through the other straw.

# 44

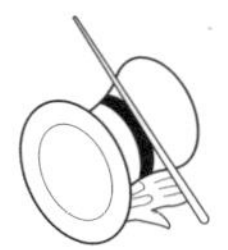

# THE HOPPING PING-PONG BALL

You need:

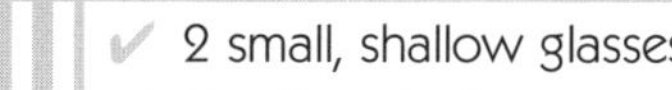

- 2 small, shallow glasses
- Ping-Pong ball

A BALL HOPS FROM ONE GLASS to another.

Place the two glasses side by side, and put a Ping-Pong ball into the one nearest you, as shown.

The challenge is to get the ball into the other cup without touching the ball in any way.

After all your friends give up trying, you show them how to do it. Simply blow on the side of the ball nearest you. With a little practice, you'll be able to make it jump from one glass into the other.

## Why does it work?

The trick works because the air you blow down the ball nearest you creates a pocket of compressed air that blows the ball up and forward.

# 45

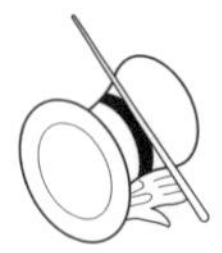

# BALLS THAT CHANGE PLACES

You need:

- a hair dryer
- 2 Ping-Pong balls

PLACE A HAIR DRYER ON THE FLOOR SO THAT ITS BLAST OF AIR is directed straight up. If you now put two Ping-Pong balls in the air stream, they will remain in the stream, as shown in the illustration opposite.

Pick up the highest ball, hold it high, and let it fall into the air stream. The two balls will change places as they remain suspended.

## Why does it work?

The balls remain suspended in the stream of air because of something physicists call "The Bernoulli Effect." Simply explained, the faster air (or water) moves, the less pressure it has. The stream of air from the hair dryer creates a column of fast moving air. The Ping-Pong balls float in this column because, while the rushing air

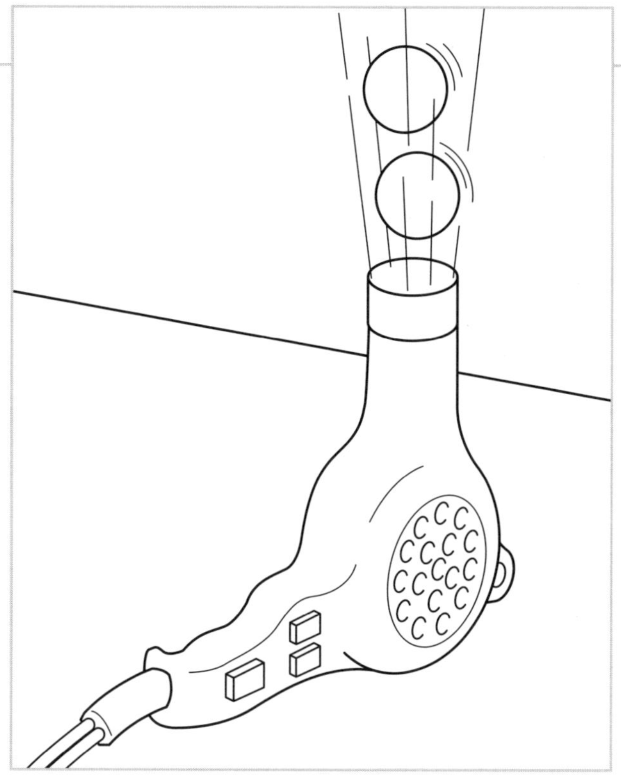

keeps them aloft, the still air surrounding the column exerts more pressure, which keeps them in place. Even if you tip the hair dryer, you'll see that the balls remain in the low-pressure stream of air, supported by the high-pressure air surrounding them!

When you pick up the highest ball and drop it, the downward force of gravity is greater than the upward rush of air—at least initially. The dropped ball falls through the column and forces its way around the floating ball. Now the upward rush of air is strong enough to cancel out the force of gravity, and the dropped ball stops falling. But the balls have changed places!

# 46

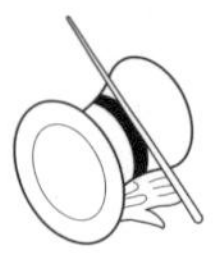

# BALLOONS THAT DON'T BURST

**You need:**

- an inflated balloon ✓
- pin ✓
- tape ✓

TELL YOUR FRIENDS THAT YOU CAN PUNCTURE A BALLOON three times without breaking it. What they don't know is that there are two spots on an inflated balloon where you can push in a pin without breaking the balloon. One spot is directly alongside the balloon's mouth. The other is directly opposite the mouth.

You can create a third spot by attaching a small piece of invisible cellophane tape on the side of the balloon. The balloon will not burst when a pin pierces the tape.

After puncturing the balloon at the three spots without exploding it, end the trick by pricking the balloon at a vulnerable spot to burst it.

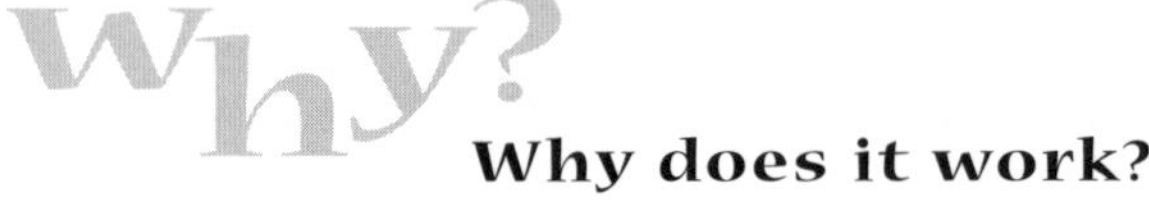


## Why does it work?

When you blow up a balloon it stretches and expands. The material it's made of gets thinner and weaker, but

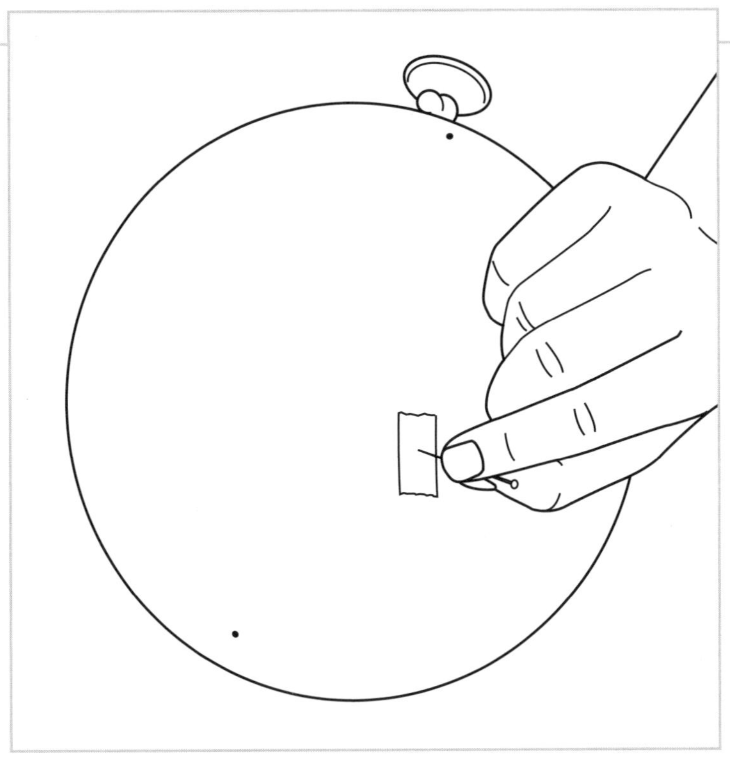

since there's an equal pull in every direction, the balloon stays together. When you stick a pin in the balloon, you make a tear in the stretched material. The rest of the balloon pulls more strongly at the edges of the tear, and it grows so rapidly the balloon bursts. But you'll notice that there are some places on a blown-up balloon where the material isn't stretched so thin. These are beside the mouth and directly opposite. When you stick a pin in here you make a tear, but the surrounding material doesn't pull very much, so it doesn't get any worse. Cellophane tape also keeps the stretched material from being pulled apart.

# 47

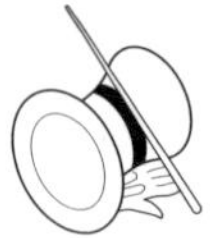

# PERPETUAL MOTION

**You need:**

- a bowl ✔
- Ping-Pong ball ✔

IS THIS PERPETUAL MOTION?

Put a Ping-Pong ball into a soup bowl and start it rolling around the rim. Everyone naturally expects it will soon stop rolling, but it continues to circle the dish for many minutes. Circle your finger around the edge of the bowl, as if you are magically keeping the ball moving.

**The Secret:** Keep your face close to the bowl as you circle your forefinger around it. As the ball comes around close to your mouth, secretly blow on it through half-opened lips. Only slight and soundless puffs are necessary.

Incidentally, this makes a startling store window display—or any other kind of display where onlookers are separated from the trick. Watchers see the ball roll

perpetually around the bowl, unaware that a fan or hair dryer is concealed behind something to provide the breeze that keeps the ball moving.

## Why does it work?

Air pressure from your mouth keeps the Ping-Pong ball moving, and centrifugal force keeps it close to the rim of the bowl. But it may take some practice to keep the Ping-Pong ball from blowing out of the bowl.

# 48

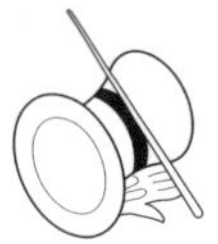

# WHIRLING CRACKERS AND PINWHEELS

**You need:**

- square soda cracker
- square of paper
- pencil with eraser

HERE ARE SOME WAYS TO MAKE OBJECTS ROTATE RAPIDLY.

Hold a square soda cracker lightly at opposite corners between the tips of your thumb and middle finger. Blow on it, and see it rotate merrily.

A whirling pinwheel is also easy to make from a 5-inch (11.25cm) square of paper, as shown in the illustration. Fold over the corners and push a pin into the eraser end of a pencil. Wave the pencil through the air to make the paper rotate.

Drag the pinwheel backward and it will spin the opposite way.

## Why does it work?

When you blow on the cracker, the air pressure you create pushes on the surface of the cracker. If the force is greater on one part—for example on the top of the cracker—that part will begin to move away from you, bringing the other parts toward you. As the force of your breath turns the cracker on its side, the thin edge presents much less resistance. If your breath was forceful enough, the cracker will easily turn past this point and present its other side. Now the force of your breath is greater at the top of the rotating cracker because it is closer to you. The cracker picks up speed as you continue to blow until it whirls merrily.

The pinwheel works in a similar way. Here, moving the pinwheel through the air creates the pressure. The force of the air on the flat surfaces of the paper is much greater than that on the thinner edge. If the pinwheel can rotate easily, and you move it quickly enough to generate sufficient momentum, it can easily overcome the resistance offered by its thinner edges and the pinwheel will pick up speed.

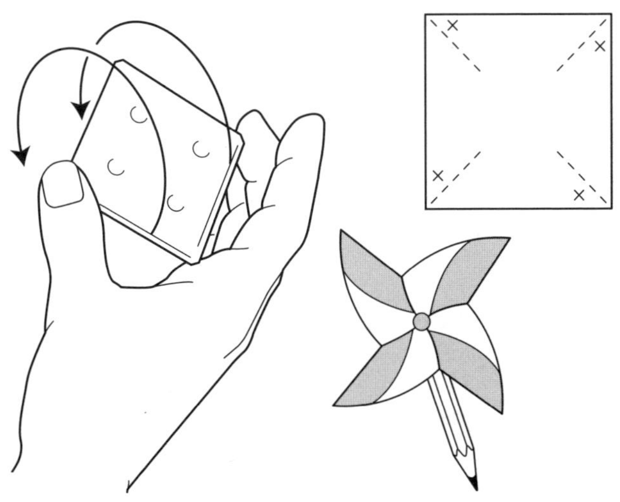

# 49

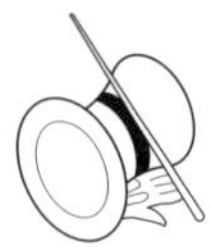

# NESTED GLASSES OR CUPS

You need:

2 glasses that can be nested (one inside the other), or plastic or Styrofoam cups

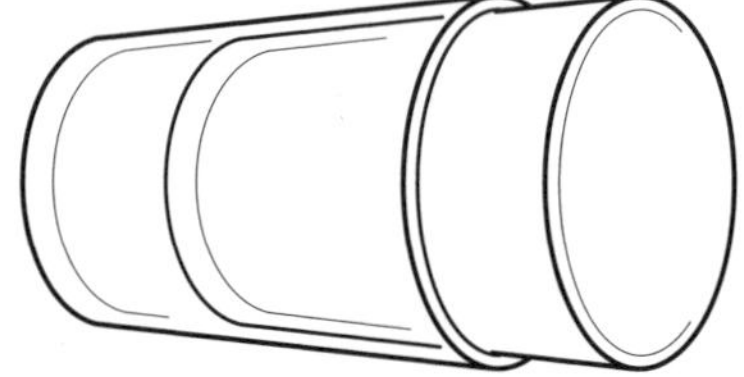

PLACE TWO NESTED GLASSES ON THEIR SIDES ON A SMOOTH table top as shown. The task is to separate the glasses without touching them in any way.

**The Secret:** Bend over and blow hard at the rim of the outer glass. Believe it or not, the air will be compressed enough inside the outer glass that the inner glass will slide free!

If you try this with a paper or Styrofoam cup, the result is even more startling. Stand the nested cups upright. Hold the bottom cup firmly while you blow at its rim. The inside cup will fly a foot or more into the air!

## Why does it work?

When you blow on the glasses, enough air goes between the rims to raise the air pressure inside the lower glass. This heightened pressure pushes the upper glass free of the lower one.

# IV.
# light and mirrors

# 50

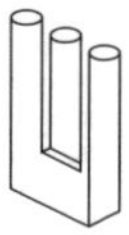

# AN APPARITION

You need:

a white wall

STARE AT THE CENTER OF THE PICTURE HERE WHILE YOU COUNT slowly to 100, then look away at a white wall. You will see a startlingly real image of Jesus!

The apparition is known as an afterimage. The retina tires of seeing black and white, and for a few moments, when you look at the wall, it reverses black and white. If you stare at a color picture, its afterimage will change the colors to their complements. Try gazing at a red apple for a minute or two, and you will see a green apple on the white wall. Stare at an orange, and you will see a blue one on the wall.

# 51

# MIRROR LEVITATION

THE NEXT TIME YOU ARE IN A DEPARTMENT STORE WHERE there are square pillars with tall mirrors on all four sides, you can astonish your friends with this amusing bit of magic.

You must be wearing a hat. Stand as shown in the illustration below so that half your body projects from the side of the mirror. The reflection of this half makes you appear normal. Your friends will now witness a seeming miracle. You appear to slowly lift both legs until you seem suspended in midair, and at the same time your hat mysteriously rises several feet above your head!

## The Secret:

What you do of course is raise your one visible leg and, with your hidden arm, lift your hat. Even adults can be totally mystified by this classic mirror illusion.

# 52

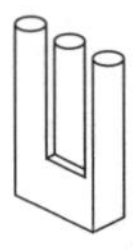

# THE UNREVERSED REFLECTION

**You need:**

- coffee mug
- paper with printing on it
- Mylar mirror paper, available at any art supply store
- glue

THE PHILOSOPHER PLATO, IN HIS DIALOGUE *TIMAEUS*, AND the later Roman poet Lucretius, in his wonderful poem about science, *On the Nature of Things*, both describe a curved mirror that refuses to reverse left and right.

(Another way to make an unreversing mirror is to place two ordinary mirrors at right angles to each other.)

I don't know who was the first person to think of the following delightful way to demonstrate the properties of such a curved mirror. You'll need a coffee mug with cylindrical sides like that in the illustration opposite. On one side of the mug, at its inside base, glue a piece of paper with printing on it. At the top of the mug, directly opposite, glue a rectangle cut from Mylar mirror paper.

When you look at the reflection of the printing in the Mylar, you'll find that the printing reads normally!

### Why does it work?

In an ordinary mirror, the light is reflected straight back at you from the same sides of the mirror, causing the image to appear reversed. In an unreversing mirror, light rays are reflected into the opposite side of the mirror before they reach you. So the image is reversed, then reversed again, and things appear as you would expect them to be. To follow the paths of reflected light rays, remember that the angle of incidence (the angle between the incoming light ray and the mirror's surface) equals the angle of reflection.

# 53

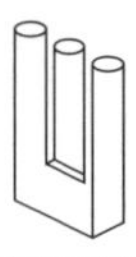

# THE REVOLVING CIRCLE

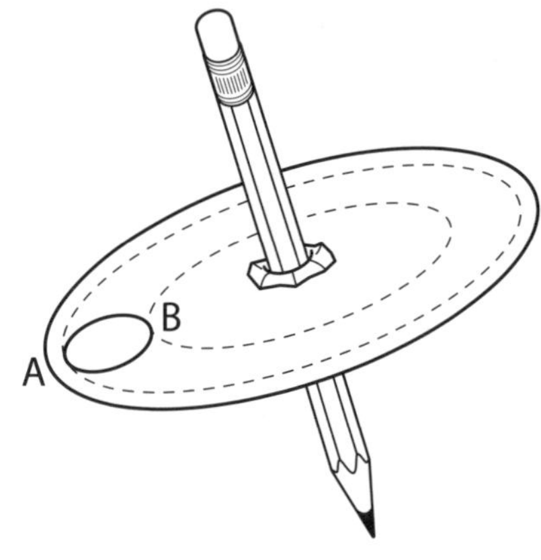


**You need:**

- white cardboard
- scissors
- sharpened pencil stub
- felt-tip pen

FROM A PIECE OF WHITE cardboard, cut a circle about six inches (15cm) in diameter. Make a hole at the center so you can push through a sharpened pencil stub to make a top. With a felt-tip pen, draw a black circle on the disk, as shown.

Can you guess what you will see when you spin the top?

**Answer:** Two small concentric circles!

### Why does it work?

The picture shows that a diameter (AB) drawn through the center of the small circle, will intersect it at two spots. When the disk is spinning, those spots travel an almost straight line compared to other points along the little circle. Thus your eyes see them for a longer period of time—long enough to generate the two large circles on the disk.

# 54

# HOW FAR APART?

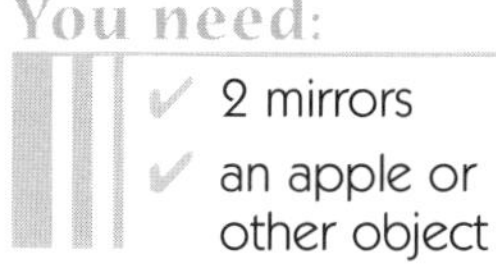


TWO MIRRORS STAND ON A COUNTER, FACING each other and situated one foot (30cm) apart. Place an object, say an apple, midway between the mirrors. Images of the apple form an endless series of reflections in the two mirrors.

The question is this: If you move the apple closer to one of the mirrors, will the two nearest images move closer together, farther apart, or remain the same? Try figuring out the answer to this puzzle before you experiment with the setup.

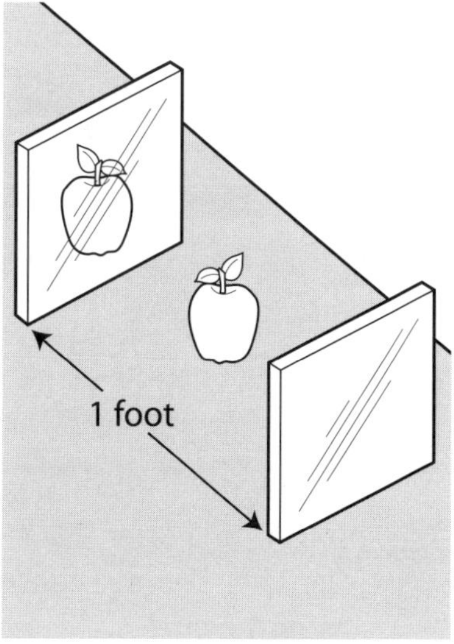


**Answer**: No matter where the apple is placed between the two mirrors, the two nearest images will always be two feet apart. Suppose, for instance, the apple is moved to one inch (2.5cm) from one mirror. Its image in that mirror will be two inches (5cm) from the apple. Its image in the other mirror will be 22 inches (55cm) from the apple. Twenty-two plus 2 equals 24 inches, or two feet (60cm)

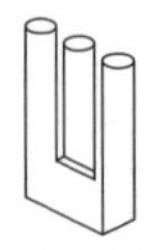

# 55

## MYSTERIOUS CIRCLES

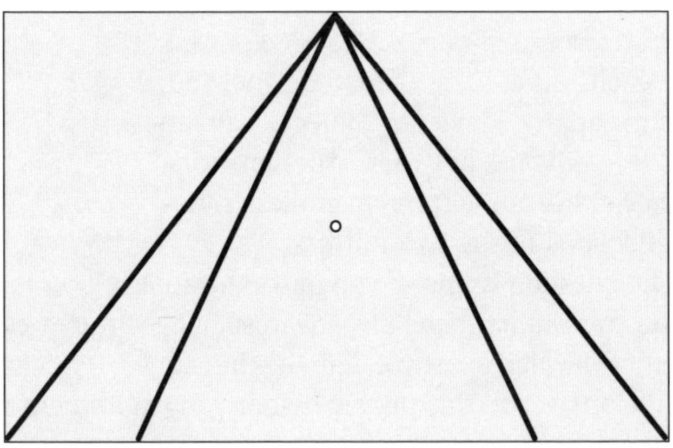

INK FOUR THICK BLACK LINES ON A FILE CARD AS SHOWN. STICK a long pin up through a hole in the card's center. Hold the pin's head beneath the card, and spin the card rapidly by flicking it with the other hand. What will you see?

You need:
- a file card ✓
- a felt-tip pen ✓
- a long pin ✓

**Answer**: Not many people can guess correctly. You will see two concentric black circles!

The explanation is the same as for "The Revolving Circle" on page 84. As the card rotates, there is a spot on each line that travels a shorter distance, compared to other spots along the line. You see those four spots a bit longer, and they form the circles.

# 56

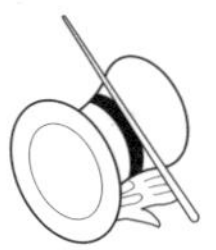

# THE BRONX CHEER EFFECT

HAVE YOU EVER BEEN SO ANNOYED BY A TV COMMERCIAL that you blew a raspberry at the set? Well, try this.

Stand as far away from the TV set as possible, then let loose with the loudest Bronx cheer that you can. You'll find that making the sound distorts the picture on the screen, so that it looks as if the vertical hold is malfunctioning!

## Why does it work?

Of course the sound has no effect on the screen. The cheer's strong vibrations rattle your eyes and produce a strobe effect that influences your vision of the screen's scanning beam. You can get the same effect with a loud humming at the right frequency.

# 57

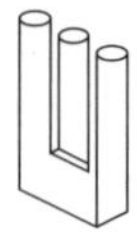

# THE VANISHING COIN

**You need:**

- a glass of water ✓
- a penny ✓
- table ✓

HERE IS A SIMPLE way to make a coin seem to disappear.

Fill a clear glass that has straight sides with water. Place it on the table. Put a coin about six inches (15cm) behind it.

When you look through the glass, you will see two coins side by side. Close either eye. One of the coins will vanish!

## Why does it work?

When light passes through the glass of water it is "refracted"—its path is bent. Refraction makes objects appear to be in a different location than they really are. In this experiment, one eye sees the coin directly, while the other sees the refracted image of the coin, which seems to be in a different location. You think you see two coins, just as you would if you crossed your eyes.

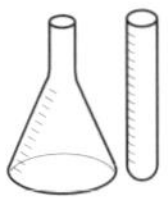

# 58

# MAKE A KALEIDOSCOPE

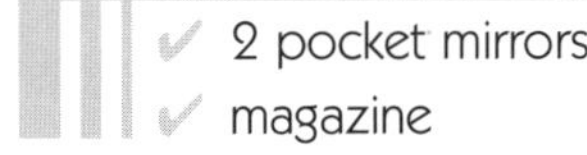


A KALEIDOSCOPE OPERATES WITH TWO mirrors that are set up at a 60-degree angle to each other. This produces a beautiful hexagonal pattern by reflecting bits of colored glass.

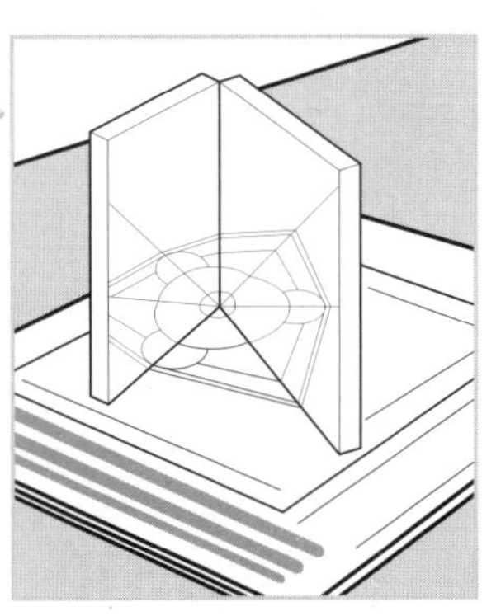

You can make a kaleidoscope with two pocket mirrors. Place them on a full-color magazine page. It's easy to adjust them to a 60° angle by looking into the mirrors and moving them until you see a reflection that has six sides, as shown in the illustration below.

Now slide the mirrors around on the page, keeping the angle fixed. You will see a constantly changing pattern identical to the changing patterns of a kaleidoscope while you keep turning it.

## Why does it work?

The 60° angle above creates a symmetrical image with six elements, each one the mirror image of that next to it. The first reflection creates a second reflection, which creates a third, and so on to the sixth reflection here. If you decrease the angle the number of reflections will increase. The image will be regular only when the angle divides evenly into 360°. This is because each regular shape that you see is made up of two mirror halves.

# 59

# TWO WAYS TO SEE YOUR THUMBPRINT

**You need:**

- a soft pencil ✓
- sheet of paper ✓
- piece of tape ✓
- glass of water ✓

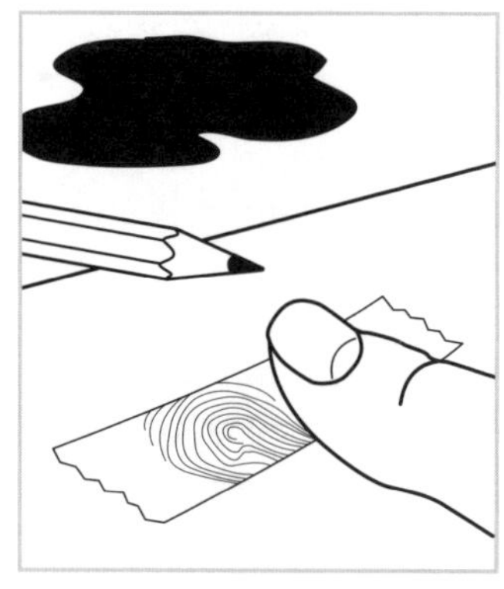

1 RUB A SOFT OR MEDIUM pencil point back and forth over a sheet of paper to make a black area of graphite. Rub your thumb over this spot to put graphite on its tip, then press the tip of your thumb against the sticky side of cellophane tape. Hold the tape up to a light to see a clear thumbprint.

2 Fill a glass with water and place it on a table. When the water is still, press your thumb firmly against the side of the glass nearest you. Bend your head until you can see the tip of your thumb through the water. Its ridges will be clearly visible.

## Why does it work?

A thumbprint consists of tiny ridges. The tape picks up the ridges more easily than the valleys between them. The same is true of the moistened side of the glass.

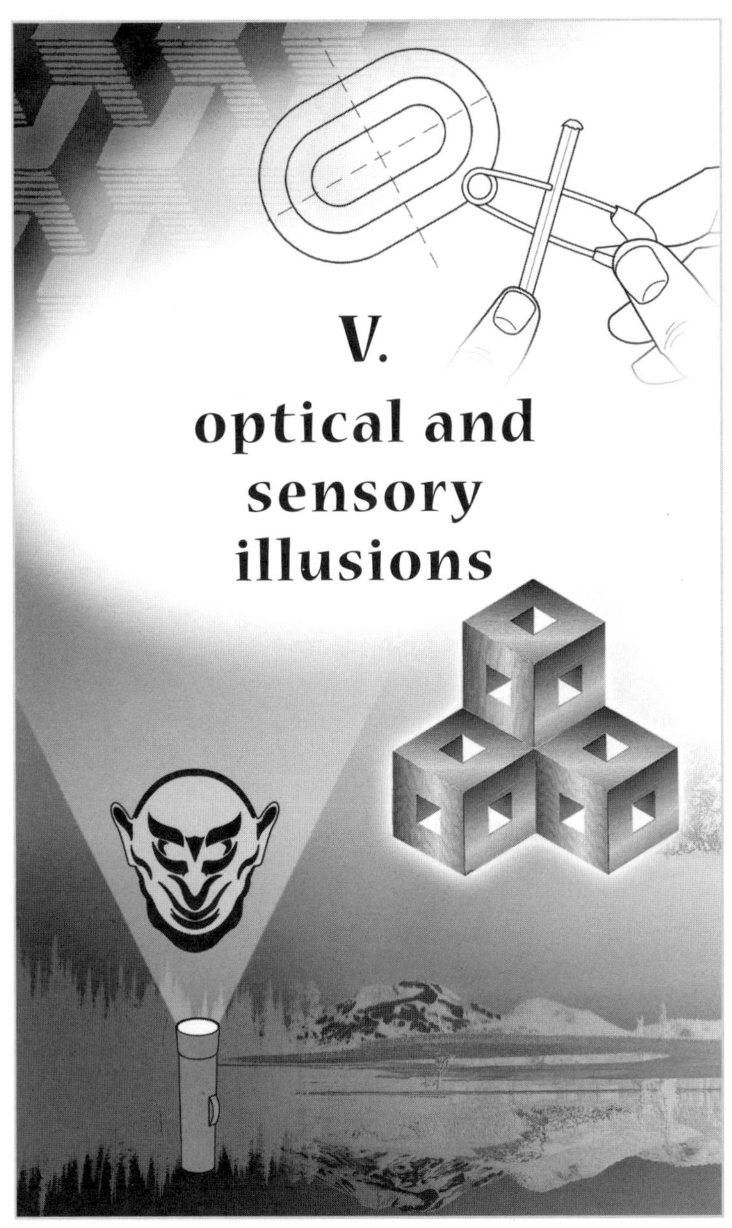

# V. optical and sensory illusions

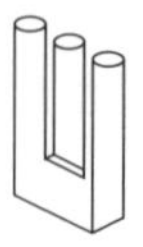

# 60

# THE ROTATING FACE

You need:

- a Halloween mask
- paint
- lamp or other light source

THIS IS A GOOD WAY TO USE A Halloween mask to make a scary optical illusion.

On the inside of a Halloween mask, use crayons or watercolors, or other kinds of paint to color the lips red, cheeks pink, and eyes blue. Darken the eyebrows. Hang the mask on a wall, painted side out. Illuminate it with light from below.

Step a few yards away. It is impossible not to see it as a normal face, instead of one turned inside out.

Now move from side to side. Horrors! The face will seem to rotate as you move! And it will seem to turn so it always faces you!

## Why does it work?

This is one of the most eerie of all optical illusions. The light from below isn't essential, but it strengthens the convexity of the mask, producing shadows where you would normally see them on a real face with light coming from above.

Because you never see a human face turned inside out, like the inside of a mask, your experience makes it impossible to see the painted mask as anything but a normal convex face. Take the face's nose, for example. If you moved right, you would see the left side of the nose. But on the inside-out mask, if you move right, you see the other side of the nose. This makes it seem as if the face is rotating. Why it seems to rotate as you move would take several pages to explain.

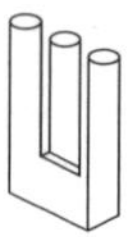

# 61

# TWO SHADES OF GRAY?

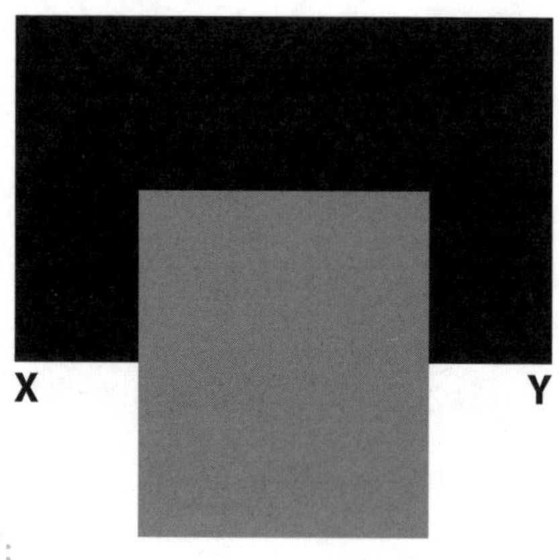


**You need:**

- this page ✔
- a pencil ✔

REST A PENCIL HORIZONTALLY ON THE LINE THAT GOES FROM X to Y in the illustration, and show it to your friends. They'll swear that the part of the gray rectangle below the pencil is a trifle darker than the part above the pencil.

Remove the pencil to show that the gray looks exactly the same throughout the rectangle.

## Why does it work?

Your eyes cannot see the subtle variation in shades of gray until a pencil marks a spot midway between the two grades.

# 62

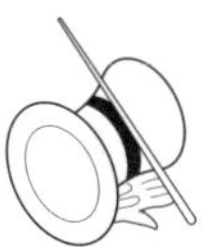

# MATCH PENETRATION

HERE IS HOW YOU CAN SEEM to make a match go through a wire.

Remove the head from a large wooden match. Push a safety pin through the match as shown in the sketch. Close the pin and hold it horizontally between thumb and forefinger. With the tip of a finger on your other hand, press firmly down on the end of the match and snap your finger off the end. The match will seem to penetrate the wire it was pressed against.

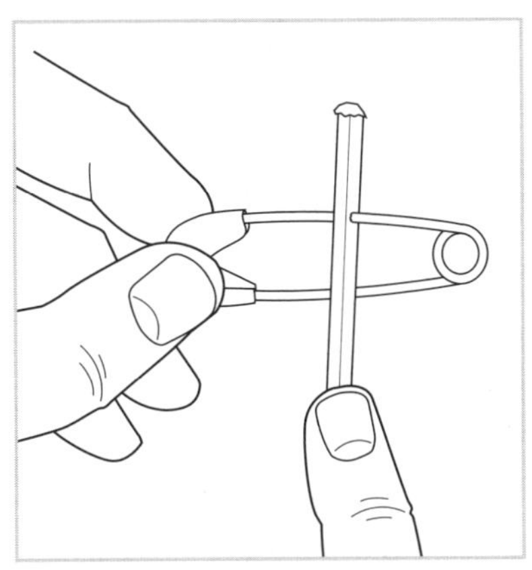

### Why does it work?

What happens of course is that the match rotates rapidly around its axis—so fast that you can't see it move. Perched owls can create a similar illusion. If you walk around the owl, it may rotate its head to follow you until its head has turned as far as it will go. The owl then snaps its head around the other way so fast that you can't see it move. It looks as though the owl has rotated its head 360 degrees.

# 63

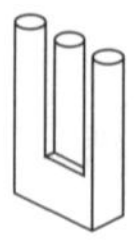

## THE TABLETOPS ILLUSION

THIS IS ONE OF THE MOST AMAZING OF ALL OPTICAL ILLUSIONS involving the comparison of shapes. It is impossible not to see the top of the table on the left as longer and thinner than the one on the right. To convince yourself that the two shapes are the same size, copy the picture on a copy machine and then cut out one of the tabletops. It will fit precisely over both the tables in the picture.

Roger Shepard, an American sociologist, invented this wonderful illusion.

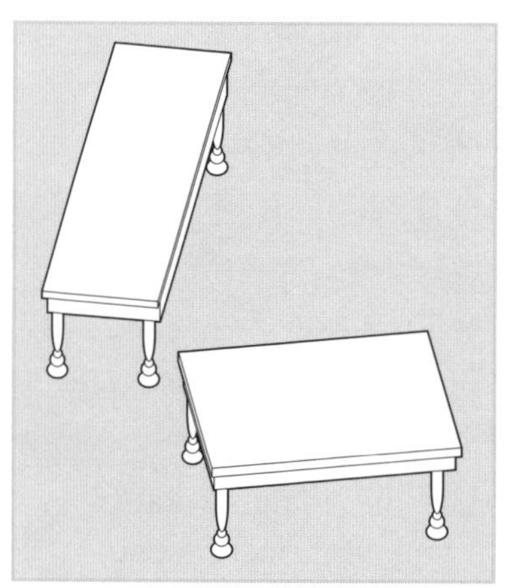

### Why does it work?

No one is really sure why this illusion works, but scientists think that the vertical tabletop appears longer than the horizontal one because its position is reinforced by the vertical orientation of the page. Some experiments suggest that our brain processes vertical arrays of visual information more easily than horizontal ones. Other theories hint that vertical sensitivity may actually be the result of how light-sensing cells are clustered together at the back of the eye.

# 64

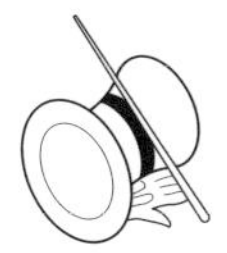

# THE AMAZING GENDER INDICATOR

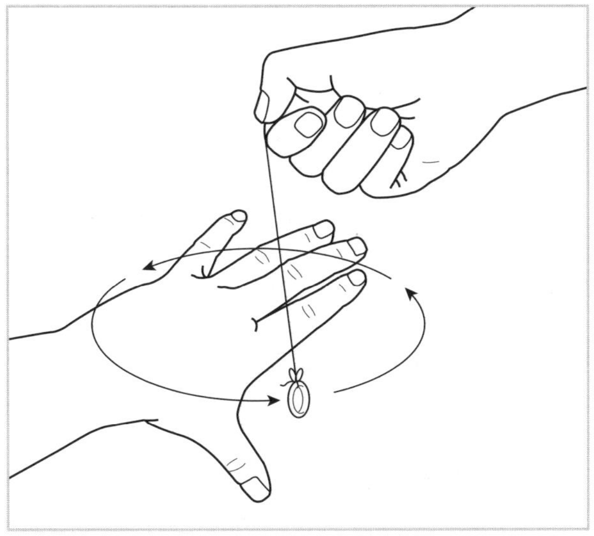

You need:

- a ring
- string

MANY DECADES AGO, NOVELTY STORES SOLD these things for a dime. You can make one in a jiffy simply by tying a small weight, such as a ring, to one end of a piece of string.

Tell someone that if she holds the free end of the strong, allowing the ring to hang suspended over a man's hand, the ring will start to swing back and forth in a straight line, like a pendulum. But if she holds the ring over a woman's hand, it will start to swing in an ellipse.

## Why does it work?

This actually works on most people no matter how hard they try to keep the ring from moving. It's a marvelous demonstration of how belief can unconsciously influence our hand.

If you find a person for whom the gender indicator works well, try this even more astonishing demonstration of how beliefs can influence hand movements. Let him hold the indicator so the ring is suspended inside a drinking glass. Tell him the ring will start moving and strike the nearest hour of the day by hitting the sides of the glass the right number of times, after which it will stop swinging. Believe it or not this, too, often works!

# 65

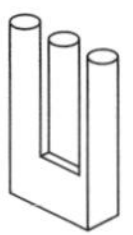

# THE AMAZING FLOATING VASE

**You need:**

- ✔ a file card

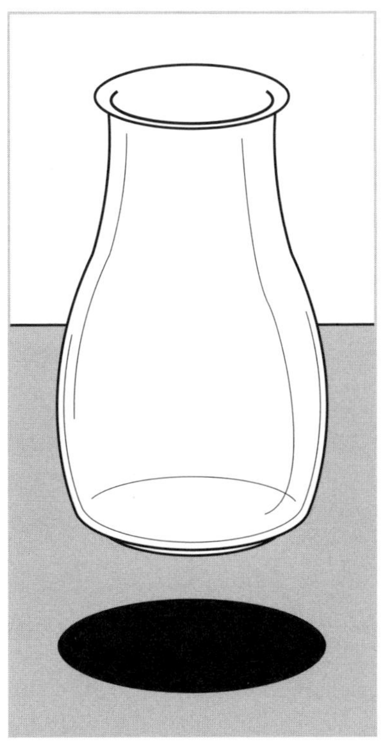

THIS REMARKABLE OPTICAL illusion illustrates how our minds make their best bet in interpreting a picture in the light of experience. This vase seems to be floating above the table. Cover the black shadow with a file card, however, and the vase will settle down on the table!

## Why does it work?

It works of course because your mind interprets the black ellipse as the shadow of a vase suspended in the air.

# 66

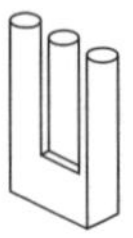

# THE FLEXIBLE OVALS

You need:

copy machine ✓
paper ✓

A VARIETY OF STRANGE OPTICAL ILLUSIONS RESULT WHEN figures are drawn on a disk and the disk is slowly rotated. Here is an example that is easy to make.

Use a copy machine to copy the square shown below with the three nested ovals. Cut out the square and crease it along both diagonals (dotted lines) to form two "valley" creases (creases that go inward when seen from above). When you open the square flat, the creases form a point at the center that will allow the square to rotate.

Place the square on a smooth, hard surface. Start it rotating very slowly with a fingertip at one corner. The concentric ovals will become deformed as if they are made of rubber.

## Why does it work?

This illusion has psychologists baffled.

One possible explanation: When you look at a TV

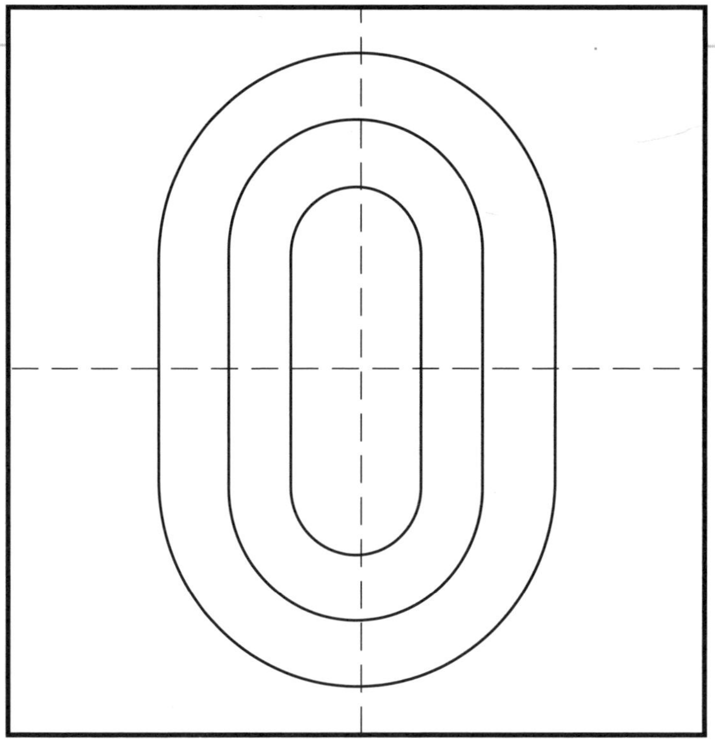

show and see a moving car or someone walking, what you're really seeing is a series of still images that change rapidly. You think you see motion because your brain takes these images and puts them all together to make a whole scene with motion. So when you look at the rotating ovals, your eyes and your brain do their best to make a scene that you can understand. The ovals don't really flex or deform, but your brain guesses that they do, since this makes the most sense given the series of images the eyes are sending it.

# 67

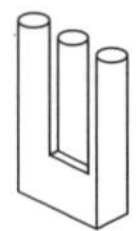

# A SPOOKY ROTATION

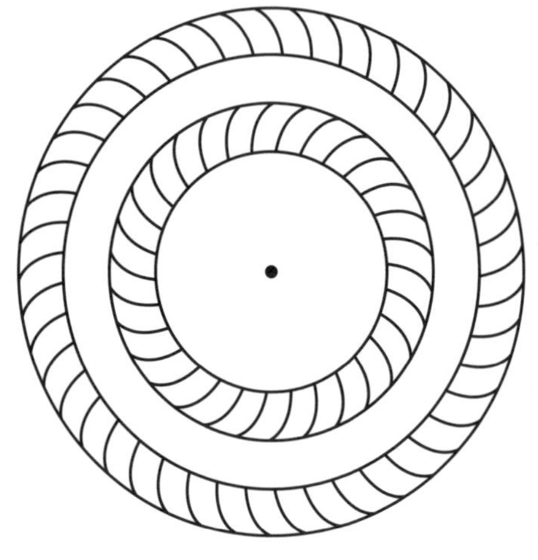

THIS AMAZING OPTICAL illusion came to me by way of Al Seckel, an expert on optical illusions.

To work the illusion, focus your attention on the central dot of the picture, then move the page slowly forward and backward. The inner wheel seems to rotate slightly counterclockwise as the page moves toward you and clockwise as the page moves away from you.

### Why does it work?

This illusion too has psychologists stumped. Scientists don't completely understand why it works either, but the explanation may be similar to what was proposed for the "Flexible Ovals" illusion. The motion of the dot and wheels towards and away from you presents your brain with a series of images that it tries to string together in a logical sequence of motion.

# 68

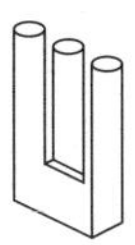

# THE VANISHING SMUDGE

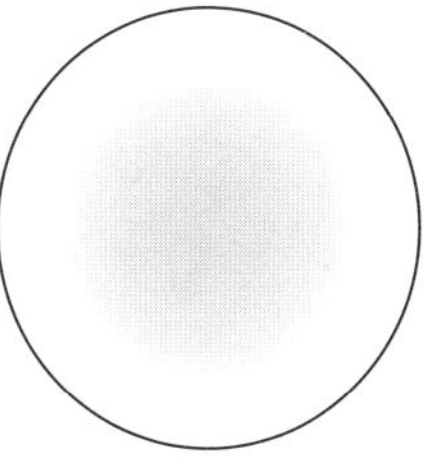

COVER ONE EYE AND STARE AT THE CENTER OF THE SMUDGE ON the left. After a few seconds, the smudge will mysteriously disappear.

Now do the same thing with the smudge on the right. For some reason, not well understood, the circle prevents the smudge from vanishing.

## Why does it work?

Staring at something long enough causes the light-sensing cells of the eyes to become exhausted and "shut off" temporarily. Moving the eye even slightly will refresh those cells. When the smudge is surrounded by a circle, your stare wavers slightly between the smudge and the circle surrounding it so that your eyes are refreshed. This keeps the smudge from vanishing.

# 69

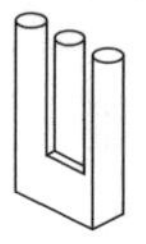

# 3-D OPTICAL ILLUSION

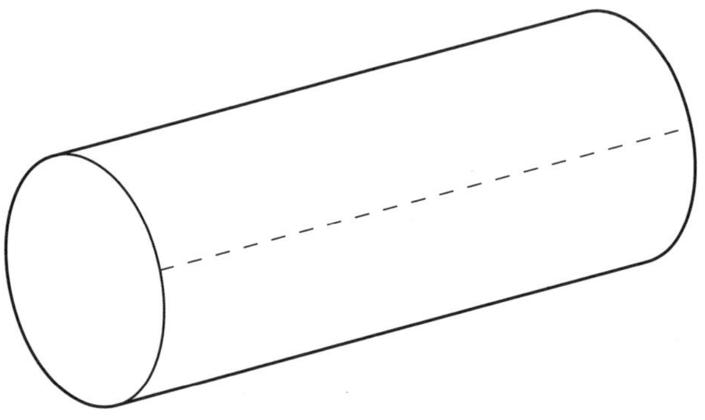

THE NEXT TIME YOU FINISH A ROLL OF TOILET PAPER, TAKE A good look at the cardboard tube. It is impossible to believe that its circumference is longer than the length of the cylindrical tube.

But it is.

**You need:**

- an empty roll of toilet paper
- scissors

Can you prove this without actually measuring the two lengths? Yes, here's how.

Cut the cylinder open along a dotted line, as shown. The resulting rectangle has one side that corresponds to the tube's circumference, and another side that is equal to the tube's length.

By folding one edge over to the top of the other edge, you will see that the tube's circumference is almost an inch longer than the tube's length!

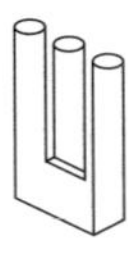

# 70

## FUNNY PENCILS

LET'S ASSUME THAT ONE OF THE TWO PENCILS YOU NEED FOR this trick is red and the other is blue. Hold the red pencil vertically and place the blue pencil horizontally on top to make a T, as shown. The red pencil will seem to onlookers considerably longer than the blue one.

Now pretend to push the red pencil down to a shorter length and to pull the blue pencil to make it longer. Make the T again, this time with the blue pencil vertical and the red one on top. The blue pencil now seems much longer than the red!

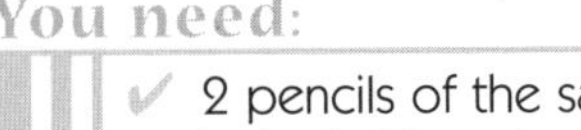

You need:

- 2 pencils of the same length but of different colors

### Why does it work?

Even this simple illusion remains mostly unexplained. But scientists suspect that the vertical pencil looks longer than the horizontal one because its position is reinforced by the vertical position of your arm and body when demonstrating this trick. In other words, the brain "extends" the length of the pencil by associating it with your arm and your body.

# 71

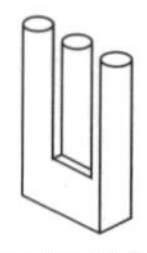

## GHOSTLY CIRCLES

Do you see dozens of little white circles in the pattern here?

Look more closely and you will realize that no circles are there! The circles are illusions, fabricated by your mind. But why are they circles instead of little white squares?

### Why does it work?

Like so many old optical illusions, this one is still far from understood. But it's probably just another example of the mind attempting to make a logical connection among multiple disconnected images. In this case, the disconnected images take the form of an interrupted pattern. The mind tries to "fill in" the missing part of the pattern to make it whole. Circles appear where the brain expects the lines of the pattern to connect into a continuous grid. But why circles? Probably because our eyes and brains are more attuned to natural shapes, like circles, than to geometrical ones, like squares.

VI.
mathematics,
sound,
physiology

# 72

# BROKEN SYMMETRY

You need:

a deck of cards
or 25 floppy disks

BROKEN SYMMETRY IS A KEY CONCEPT IN MODERN cosmology. Immediately after the Big Bang, matter was in a highly symmetrical and extremely hot state. As the universe cooled, various symmetries were broken to form the cool universe we know and love.

Here is a dramatic way to model broken symmetry. Start by balancing the cards of a deck on their edges to form the structure shown in Figure 1. You have to be very careful and patient through this process, and the assistance of a friend can be a big help. (Using 25 or so 3.5-in computer diskettes may be easier.) The completed structure has what mathematicians call "radial symmetry," like the symmetry of a right circular cylinder. It is identical with its mirror image.

Bang your fist on the table to represent the universe's Big Bang. The beautiful radial symmetry is broken, and the cards collapse into the lovely rosette shown in Figure 2.

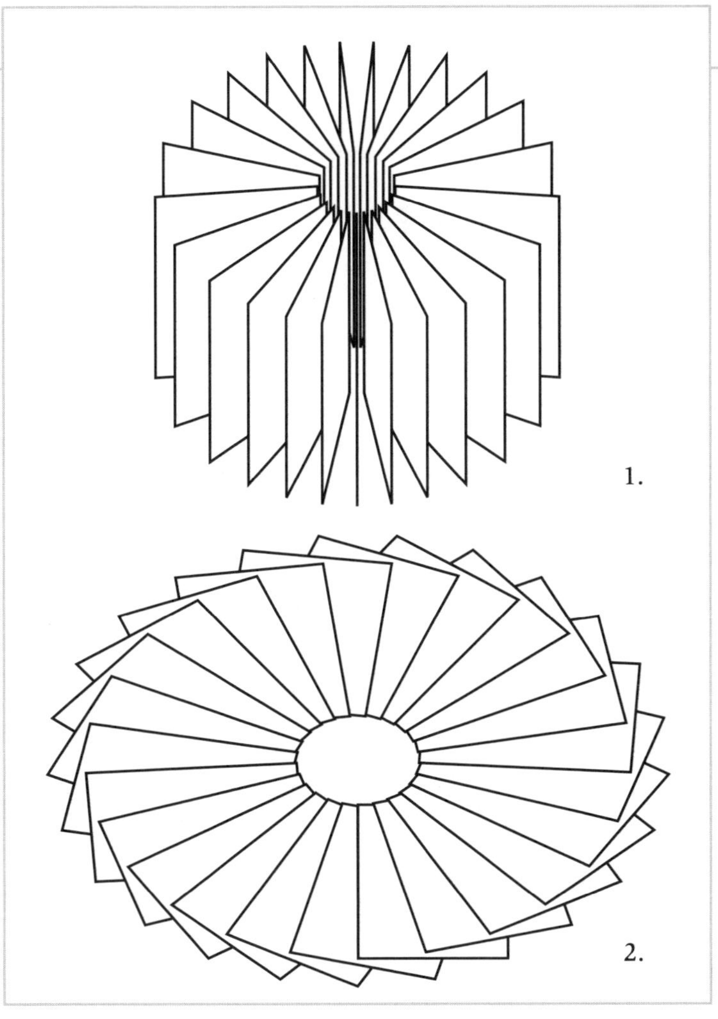


It will have left- or right-handedness (or chirality, as physicists prefer to say). The two possible states of the rosette occur with equal probability. They model the fact that as the universe cooled, its initial symmetry broke into matter rather than antimatter of opposite chirality. Exactly how and why this happened is still controversial.

# 73

# THREE SWITCHES PUZZLE

THREE ON-OFF SWITCHES ARE ON THE WALL OF A FIRST FLOOR. Call them A, B, and C. You know when each switch is on or off. One switch operates a bulb in a lamp on the third floor. The other two switches are dummies, not connected to anything. You don't know which switch operates the bulb.

You are allowed to toggle the switches any way you please. You then walk just once to the third floor where you inspect the bulb. You immediately know which switch is connected to it. How do you know?

**Answer:** Set the switches to off, then turn on a switch, say B, and leave it on for ten minutes. Turn it off, then turn on, say C. Walk to the third floor. If the bulb is warm, you know it is controlled by B. If it is cold but on, it is connected to C. If it is cold but off, the switch is A.

# 74

# THE TWO SQUARES

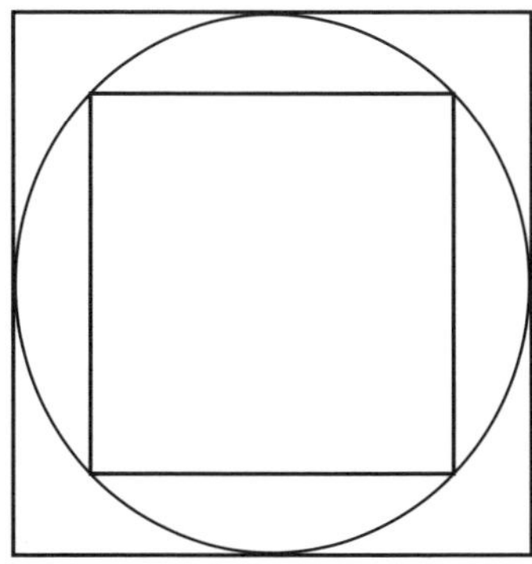

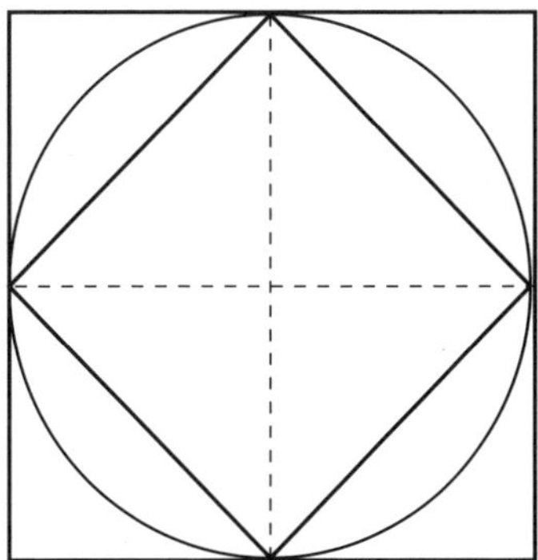

I KNOW OF NO MATH PROBLEM THAT BETTER ILLUSTRATES HOW A flash of intuition—an aha!—will provide a quick proof.

I assert that the area of the larger square is exactly twice the area of the smaller one (Figure 1). Am I right?

**Answer**: There is no need to make tedious calculations. Simply rotate the inner square in your mind to the position shown in Figure 2, and you see at once—mathematicians call this a "look-see" proof—that the inner square is indeed half the area of the outer square.

75

# FUN WITH A MÖBIUS STRIP

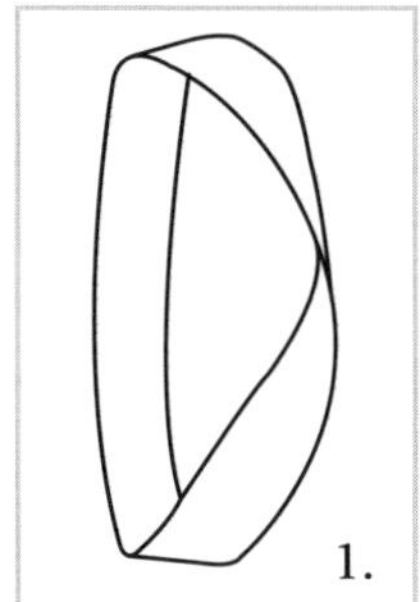
1.

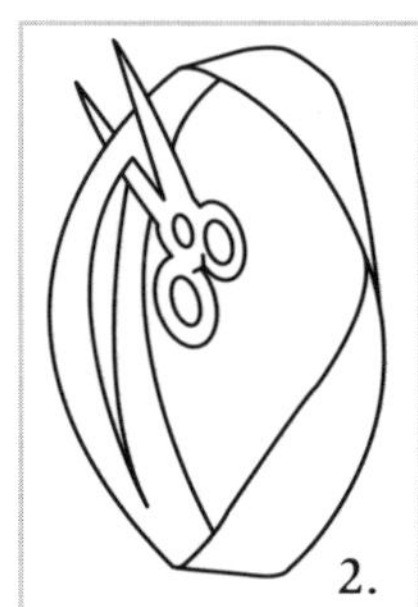
2.

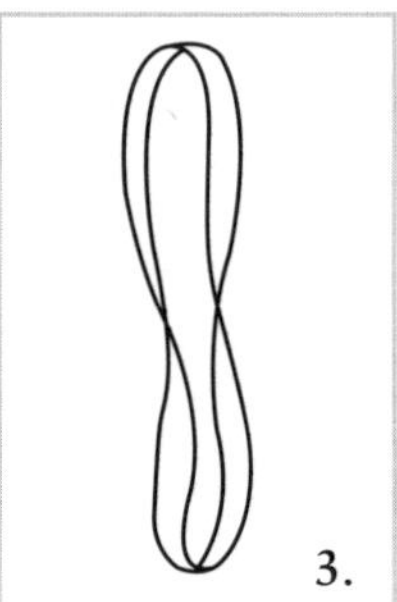
3.

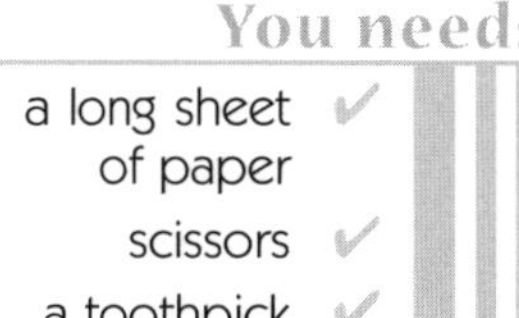


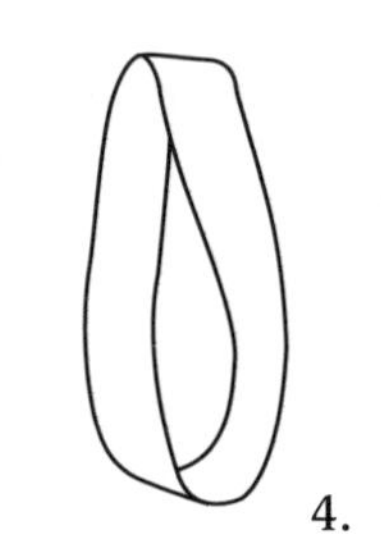
4.

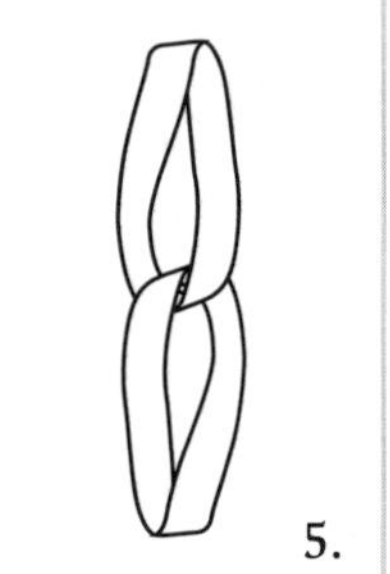
5.

GIVE A PAPER STRIP A HALF TWIST AND TAPE THE ENDS together. The result is called a Möbius strip (Figure 1). You can easily verify that the strip has only one side and only one edge. If you cut the strip in half lengthwise (Figure 2), the result is not two strips, as you might expect, but one large strip with a double twist (Figure 3). If you make a second strip with a full twist, it is no longer one-sided (Figure 4). Cutting it in half lengthwise produces two strips of the same size—linked together (Figure 5).

Make a third strip with a half twist. Cut this strip lengthwise as before, but start the cut close to the edge so that you cut twice around the strip instead of once around. Result? One large strip with a small strip linked through it.

Cut two identical strips of paper. Place one strip on top of the other, give them a half twist, and join the ends with tape. You have produced what mathematicians call a "covering" of a Möbius strip. The space between the two strips is a Möbius surface. You can insert a toothpick between the two strips and run it all the way around and back to where you started. This seems to prove that there are two separate strips. But slide the covering from the strip and you'll find there is just one strip. Now try to put the strips back together. It's not easy!

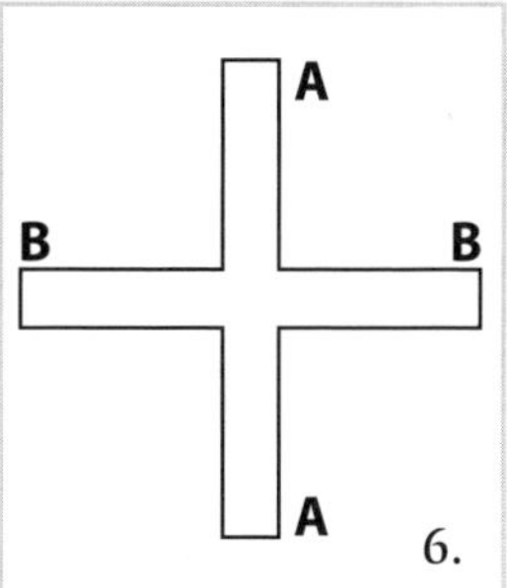

6.

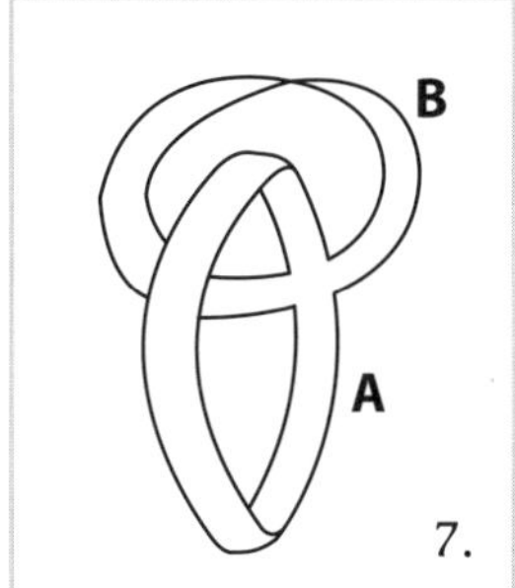

7.

8.

For a final experiment, cut a paper cross, as shown in Figure 6. Join ends A to make a strip with no twists. Join ends B to make a strip with a half twist. Figure 7 shows the result. Cut the twisted strip (B), starting the cut close to the edge, so that you cut around the strip twice. Cut the untwisted strip (A) in half lengthwise. Pull the two strips apart. The result (Figure 8) will amaze you!

# 76

# TURNING A TRIANGLE UPSIDE DOWN

**You need:**
10 pennies ✓

ARRANGE TEN PENNIES IN THE TRIANGULAR FORMATION shown below. The task is to move just three pennies that will turn the triangle upside down.

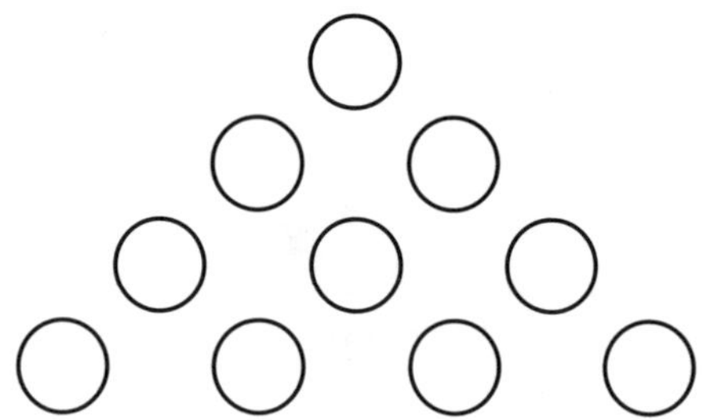

**Answer:** See page 117.

# 77

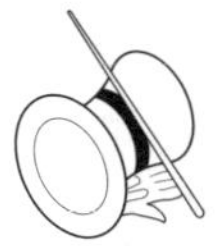

# KNOT A PENTAGRAM

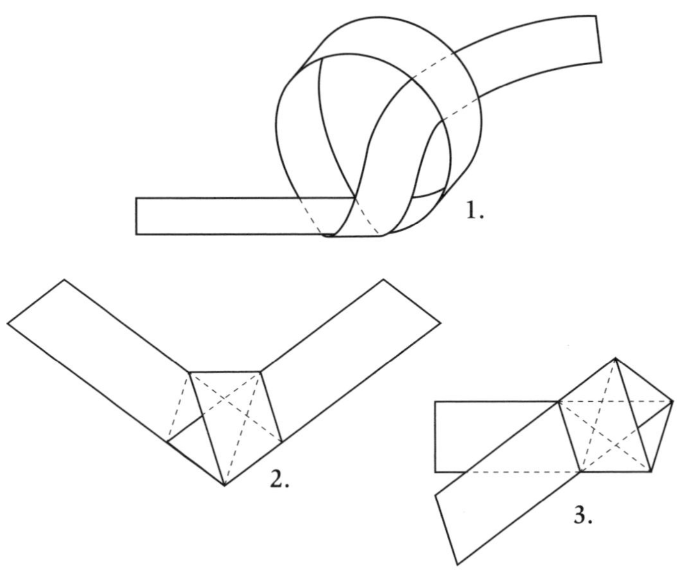


FROM THE SIDE OF A SHEET OF typewriter paper, cut a strip one inch (2.5cm) wide. Tie an overhand knot in the strip's center, as shown in Figure 2. Pull the knotted strip taut and flatten it.

**You need:**

- a sheet of typewriter paper
- scissors
- light source

Fold end A over the knot as in Figure 2.

Hold the knot up to a light. You'll see a perfect five-pointed star inscribed in a regular pentagon. It has many remarkable mathematical properties.

# 78

# PAPER CUP TELEPHONE

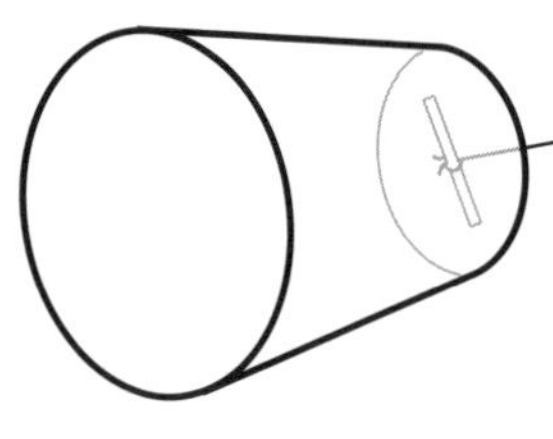

**You need:**

- 2 paper cups
- a long piece of string
- 2 toothpicks or wooden matches

MAKE A TINY HOLE AT THE BOTTOM OF ONE CUP, INSERT ONE end of the string. Inside the cup, tie the string to the middle of a wooden match or toothpick. Do the same with the other end of the string inside the other cup. The string should be long enough to allow two people to stand far apart, keeping the string taut. The match or toothpick must press firmly against the bottom of each cup.

One person speaks into a cup while the other person holds the other cup to her ear. The string will transmit the vibrations produced at the bottom of the cup held by the speaker. The words will be heard distinctly by the person listening at the other end of the taut string.

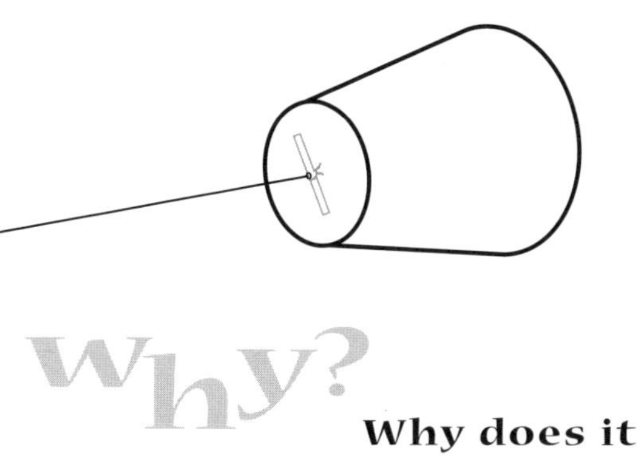

## Why does it work?

The bottom of a cup works like the diaphragm of a microphone or a speaker. Sound causes a microphone's diaphragm to flex back and forth, or vibrate, and the same thing happens to the bottom of the paper cup. In this experiment, vibrations are carried along the string, but in a real telephone, the diaphragm's vibrations are converted into electrical impulses that are sent through a wire. At the other end, both the electrical impulses and the string's vibrations are converted back into sound by causing another diaphragm to flex back and forth in just the same way.

Solution to puzzle 76 on page 114

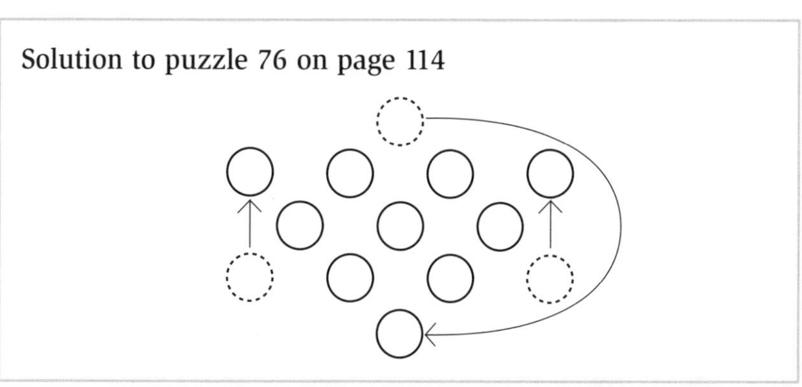

# 79

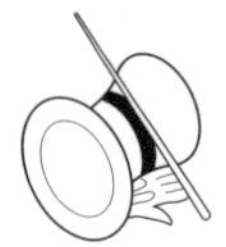

# PAPER CUP SQUAWKER

You need:

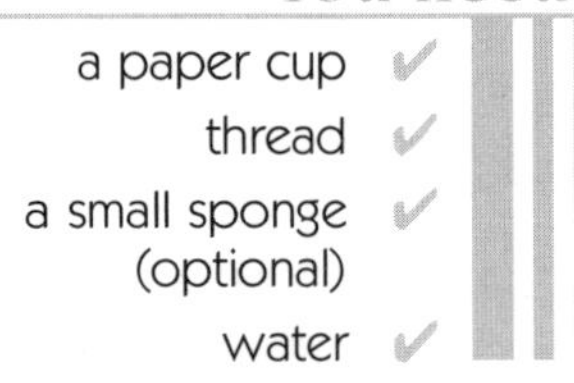


PUNCH A TINY HOLE AT THE BOTTOM of a paper cup. Run a thread through the hole and tie a knot at one end as shown. If you like, you can ink a face on the cup.

Hold the cup in one hand, wet the fingers of your other hand, and pinch the hanging thread just below the cup, then slide down the thread. Better yet, pinch the thread with a small wet sponge and slide it down. The cup will make an amazingly loud squawking sound!

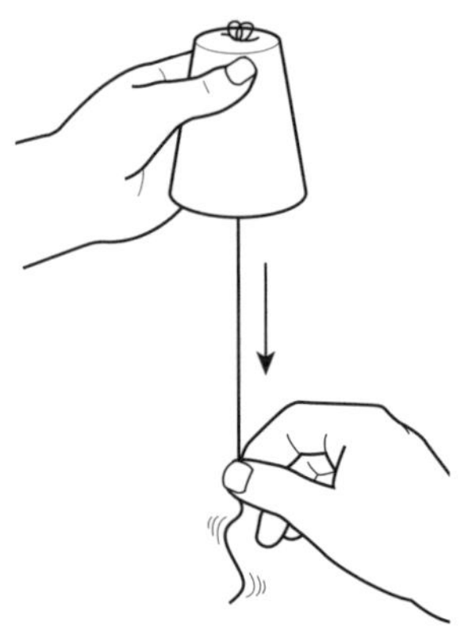

## Why does it work?

A wet sponge or fingers have just the right amount of friction against the thread. So as you slide the sponge or your fingers down, the thread is quickly caught and released many times a second. This makes the string vibrate rapidly and that, in turn, makes the bottom of the cup vibrate. When the cup bottom vibrates, quickly flexing back and forth, this makes the air vibrate, which you hear as a very loud squawking sound. The sides of the cup act like a megaphone and help direct and amplify the sound.

# 80

# THE VIBRATING CARD

THE SOUND PRODUCED BY A CLARINET, saxophone, or any other reed instrument, is caused by the vibration of a reed. The sound of wind instruments, such as a cornet or trombone, is produced by vibrating air. With instruments like violins or cellos, the friction of the bow against a string causes the sound. The faster the vibrations, the higher the pitch of the sound.

**You need:**

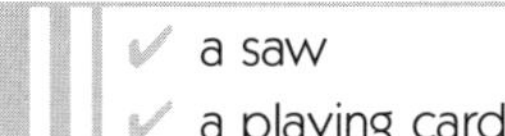

- a saw
- a playing card

A simple demonstration of all this is to run the edge of a playing card over the teeth of a saw. The movement of the card produces a low sound in the saw that rises in pitch when you move the card faster.

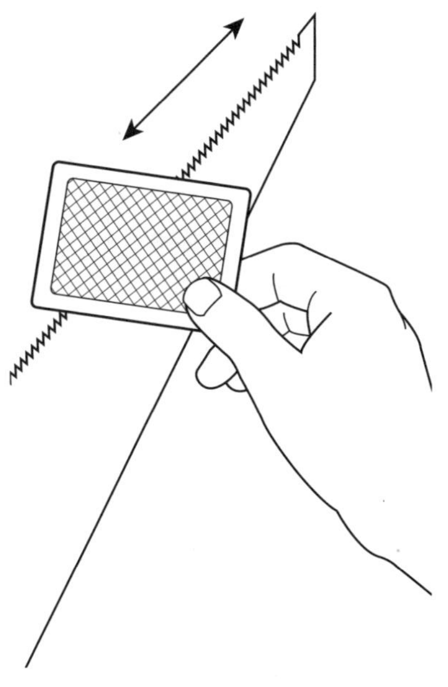

## Why does it work?

The friction of the card against the edge of the saw is similar to that of a bow against a violin string. Vibrations are created in the saw that resonate throughout its body, causing the saw to "sing."

# 81

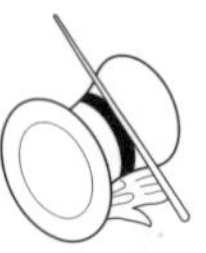

# A PAPER POPPER

**You need:**

- a single page of newspaper

IN HIS DIARY, LEWIS CARROLL, AUTHOR OF *ALICE IN Wonderland*, speaks of making what he called "paper pistols" for his child friends. The "pistol" is best folded from a single sheet of newspaper as shown in the illustrations. When held at one corner and swung rapidly through the air, a portion of the paper pops out with a bang.

Fold the paper in half lengthwise and crosswise and open it up flat. Fold the corners at the longest end down to the lengthwise fold line and then fold the whole in half so the folded corners are on the inside. It should look like Figure 3. Fold the outer corners down toward you to the midline so it looks like Figure 4. Turn the packet over (Figure 5) and fold it toward you in half along the midline. Hold the popper (Figure 6) at the bottom and pop.

## Why does it work?

The bang is produced by the rapid popping out of a folded part of the paper, which catches the air as you swing the popper. It is similar to the sound of a popped paper bag.

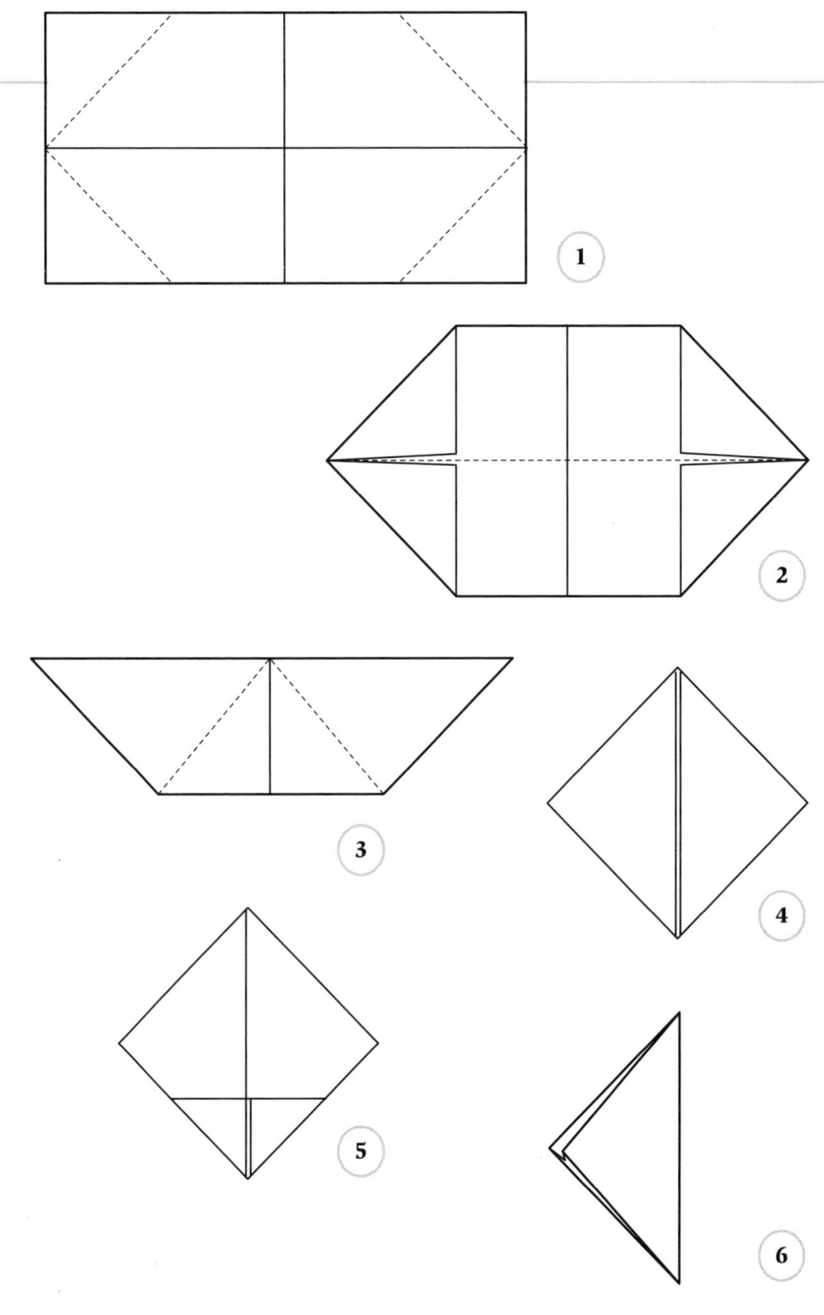
1
2
3
4
5
6

# 82

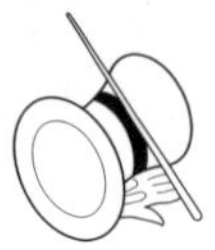

# STOP YOUR PULSE!

**You need:**
a handkerchief

TIE A FEW TIGHT KNOTS IN A handkerchief and secretly place it in one of your armpits, where it is hidden by your clothing. Let someone feel your pulse at the wrist of the same arm. Tell her that at the count of three, you will cause your pulse to stop. Sure enough, it does!

## Why does it work?

To stop your pulse, simply press your arm against the knotted cloth. Pressure on the arm's main artery will lower your pulse to a beat that cannot be felt. After a moment or two, snap your fingers to release the pressure, and "command" your pulse to return.

# 83

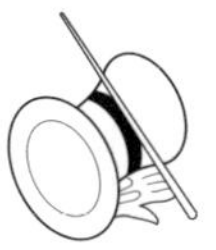

# FIND THE PENNY

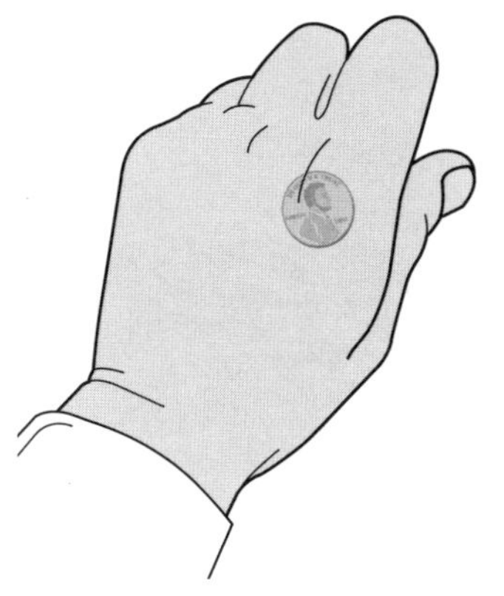

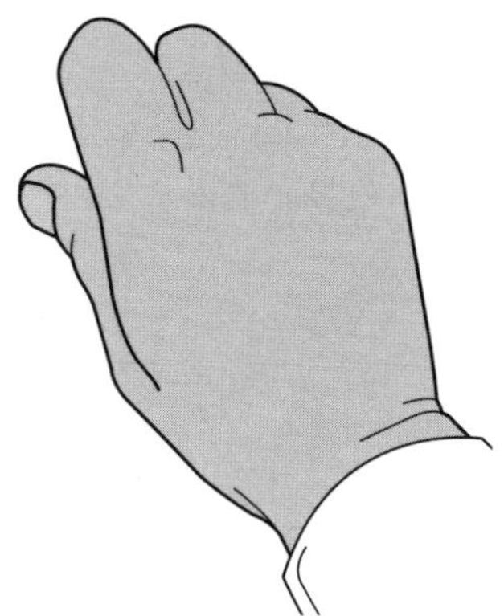

**You need:**

✓ a penny

WHILE YOUR BACK IS TURNED, ASK SOMEONE to hold a penny inside the fist of either hand. Tell him to hold the hand with the penny high above his head, while he counts to fifty, then lower it.

Turn around. Ask him to extend both fists, with the back of his hands up, and you will try to guess which hand holds the penny. Each time you repeat this trick you guess the hand correctly.

## The Secret:

While the arm is raised, gravity causes the blood in the veins of the hand to flow downward. This makes the back of the hand that was held up a trifle lighter than the back of the other hand.

# 84

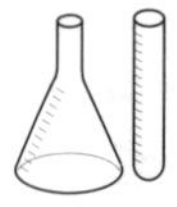

# IT'S NOT EASY!

**You need:**

- pencil or pen ✓
- paper ✓

SEE IF YOU CAN WRITE YOUR NAME while at the same time you move one foot in horizontal circles. Try it. It's impossible!

### Why does it work?

Your brain isn't able to keep your foot turning properly and at the same time tell your hand how to write your name.

VII.
electricity,
magnetism,
gravity

# 85

# WHICH IS WHICH?

You need:

2 magnets ✓

SUPPOSE YOU ARE HANDED TWO IDENTICAL IRON BARS, A and B, and told that one of them—and only one—is a magnet. Without being allowed to touch a bar to any metal that would give it away, how can you tell which bar is the magnet?

### Answer:

Touch the end of the bar, say A, to the middle of bar B. If there is attraction, then A is the magnet. Otherwise, B is the magnet.

### Why does it work?

All magnets have two poles, a north pole and a south pole. The north pole of a magnet will attract the opposite, south pole of another magnet and will repel the similar, north pole of another magnet. Either pole will attract an ordinary, un-magnetized bar of metal. In the middle of a magnet, between the poles, the north and south forces cancel each other out. So at this point there is no magnetic force to attract the metal bar or to attract or repel another magnet.

# 86

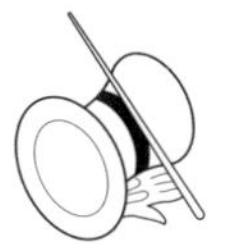

# THE SUSPENDED PENCIL

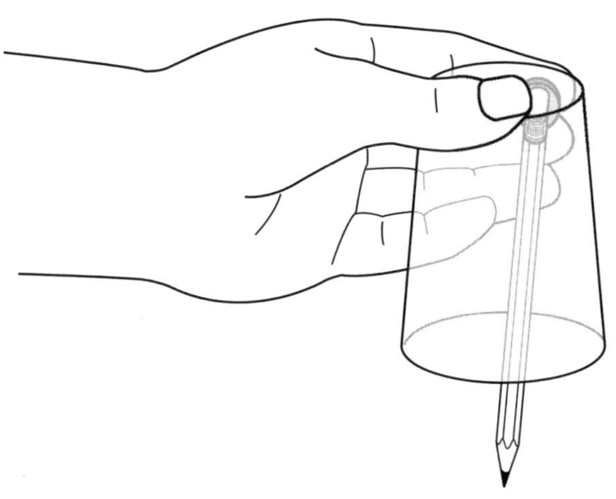

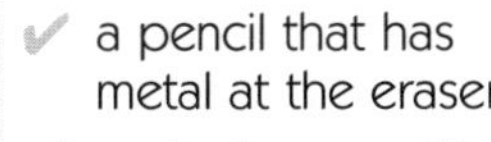

You need:

- a pencil that has metal at the eraser
- a plastic cup with opaque sides
- small magnet

HOLD THE CUP UPSIDE DOWN, with a small magnet concealed under your fingers.

With your other hand, push the eraser end of the pencil up into the cup on the side where the magnet is hidden. Remove the hand holding the pencil. The pencil will remain mysteriously suspended. Be sure the magnet is on your side of the cup, where it can't be seen.

Remove the pencil. As you place the cup and pencil on the table, secretly remove the magnet. Now people can examine the cup and the pencil without their revealing how the trick works.

Instead of a cup you can use a cardboard tube such as the one inside toilet paper rolls.

## Why does it work?

The magnet attracts the metal in the band that holds the pencil's eraser, and this will keep the pencil suspended. The force of a magnet is able to easily penetrate a plastic cup or cardboard tube. In fact, a strong magnetic force can penetrate much thicker or more solid objects than these.

# 87

# KNOCK OFF THE MATCH

CAREFULLY BALANCE A COIN ON its edge and put a paper match on top of it, as shown. Place an empty glass upside down over the coin and match.

**You need:**

- a coin
- a paper match
- transparent plastic cup
- pocket comb

**The problem:** Knock the match off the coin without causing the coin to topple over. You are not allowed to touch the glass in any way. Banging the table won't do it, because it would cause the coin to fall.

**The Secret:** Static electricity does the trick. Rub a pocket comb briskly on your clothing and hold the comb close to the glass. The match will fall, leaving the coin still balanced on its edge, undisturbed.

# 88

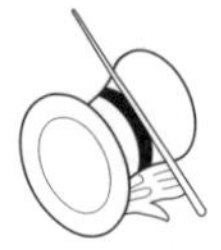

# A CRAWLING PAPER CLIP

**You need:**

- a magnet ✓
- low table with a thin top ✓
- sheet of white paper ✓
- paper clip ✓
- compass (optional) ✓

SECRETLY TAPE A MAGNET TO THE TOP OF ONE KNEE, WHERE it will be concealed by your clothing. Sit at a table that has a thin top and is low enough for you to bring the magnet on your knee to the underside of the table.

Place a sheet of white paper on the table. On the sheet, put a paper clip. By moving your knee under the table, you can make the paper clip seem to come alive and crawl like a little bug here and there across the paper!

You can influence a compass needle the same way. Put the compass on the table and pretend to be psychically influencing its needle. Wiggling your magnet underneath the table will of course cause the compass needle to gyrate back and forth as if you are doing this with a "mysterious" force unknown to science.

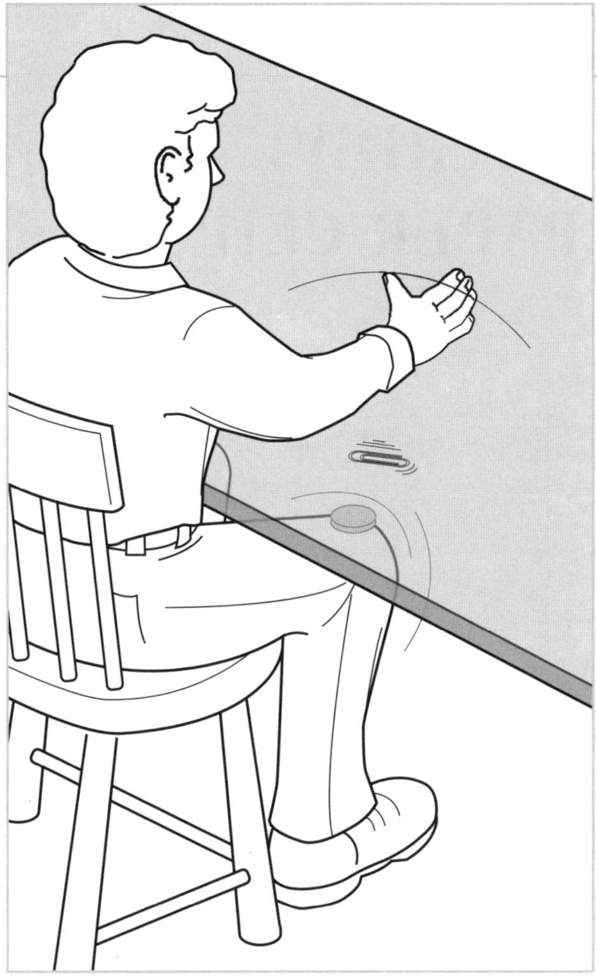

## Why does it work?

Magnetic force is able to penetrate many solid objects, including paper.

# 89

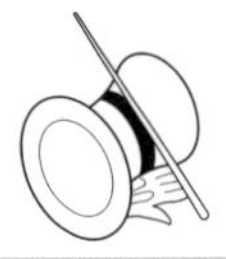

# RETRIEVE THE PAPER CLIP

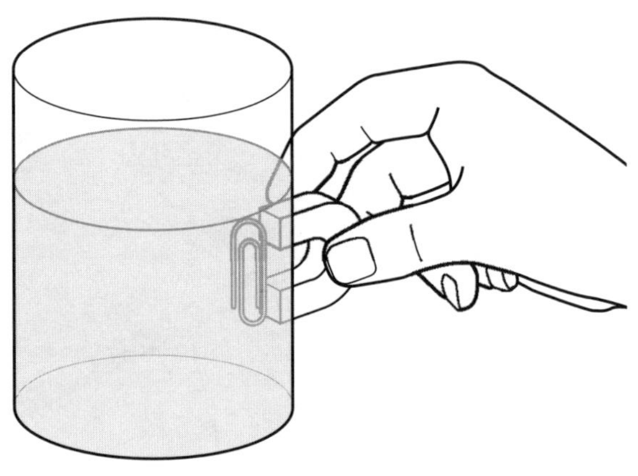

DROP A PAPER CLIP INTO ANY EMPTY LARGE GLASS OR plastic bottle, and then fill the bottle with water.

How can you get the clip out of the bottle without emptying the water or getting your fingers wet?

**You need:**

- a paper clip ✓
- a large glass or plastic bottle ✓
- water ✓
- magnet ✓

**The Secret:** Slide the magnet up along the outside of the bottle, carrying the clip up and out of the bottle's mouth.

## Why does it work?

Magnetic force is able to penetrate many solid objects, even glass!

# 90

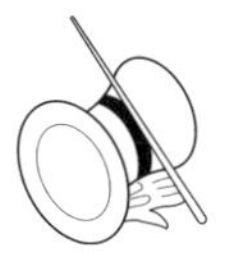

# THE PAPER CLIP CHAIN

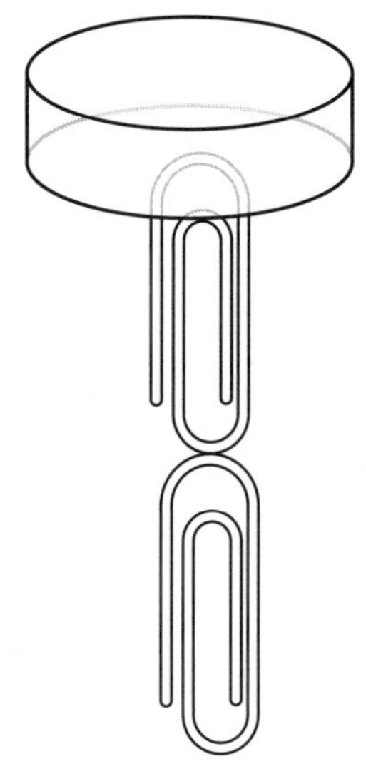

IT'S EASY TO HANG A PAPER CLIP on the bottom of a magnet, as shown. With a little more care you can suspend a second clip under the first.

After you have the two paper clips connected, carefully lift away from the magnet the top clip of the chain. Once it is away from the magnet, will the second clip drop free?

Surprisingly, it will not!

More powerful magnets will support a chain of three or more paper clips.

**You need:**

- ✓ 2 paper clips
- ✓ a magnet

## Why does it work?

The atoms in most objects have a tiny amount of magnetic force, but because their poles are not aligned with each other, these forces cancel each other out. In a magnet, many more atoms are aligned, so they work together to create a greater force overall. A magnet also has the ability to "induce" the same alignment in certain types of objects, such as a metal paper clip.

# 91

# THE BALL THAT ROLLS UPHILL

**You need:**

- 2 new wooden pencils ✓
- a deck of cards ✓
- a Ping-Pong ball ✓
- a book ✓

DIVIDE THE DECK IN HALF, PLACING THE HALVES SIDE BY SIDE. Place the pencils on the half-decks, with eraser ends touching and other ends on the table about 1¼ inches (3.12cm) apart (Figure 1). Put the Ping-Pong ball at the center of the V to show how it will roll downhill and off the pencils onto the table.

Move the half-decks so they also are 1¼ inches (3.12cm) apart, as shown in Figure 2. Rearrange the pencils so their eraser ends touch the table, and their other ends are 1¼ inches (3.12cm) apart, each resting on the inside edge of a half-deck. Put a weight (the edge of a book will do) on the eraser ends to hold them firmly in place. Put the ball in the middle of the pencils as shown. Which way will it roll? Because the cards are raising the ends of the pencils ¼ inch (6.25mm), people are likely to

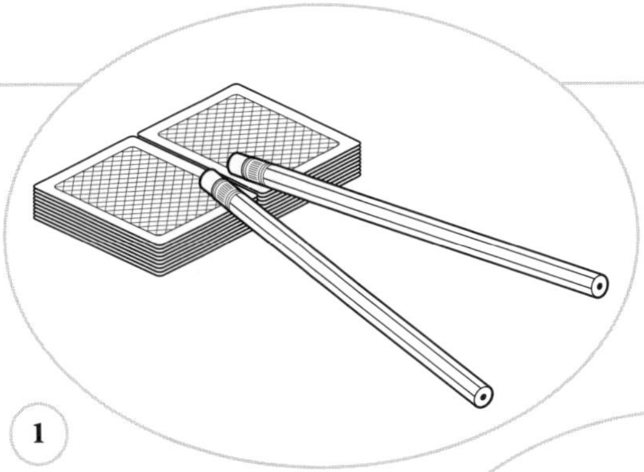

1

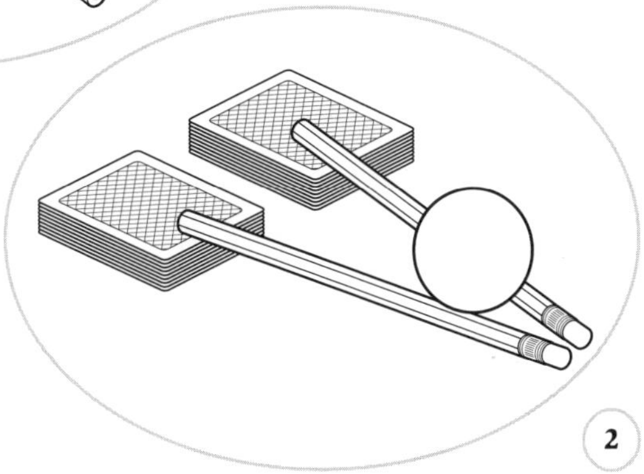

2

guess that the ball, as before, will roll toward the pencils' lower ends.

Surprisingly, it doesn't! It seems to roll uphill toward the pencils' higher ends!

## Why does it work?

Actually, the ball's center of gravity lowers as it moves toward the open end of the V, so it is really rolling downhill.

92

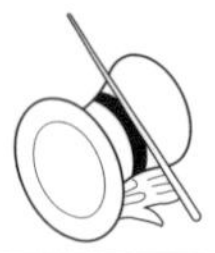

# MOVING AN OBJECT WITH YOUR MIND

You need:

a playing card

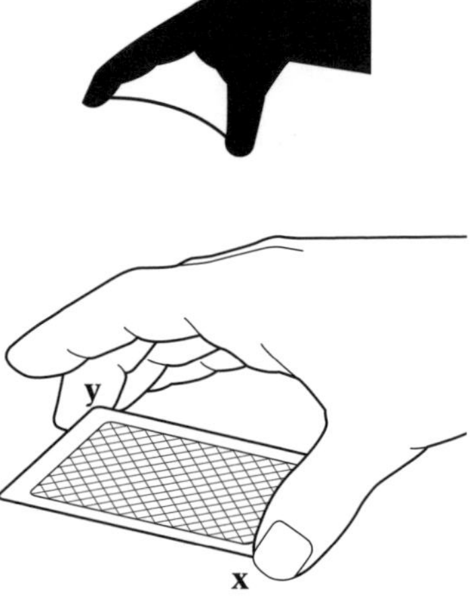


SECRETLY BEND A PLAYING card ever so slightly to make its back convex, as in the illustration. Hold the card, back side up, between the tips of your right thumb and middle finger: thumb at corner X and middle finger at Y.

Release the pressure on these diagonally opposite corners until the card is almost ready to drop to the floor. You'll find that the card will slowly turn in your hand until it's face up.

It takes a bit of practice to hold the card lightly enough to allow it to rotate. The movement is very spooky!

## Why does it work?

The bend in the card raises its center of gravity. This center always seeks its lowest point, and in doing so, causes the card to turn.

# 93

# A PECULIAR BALANCE

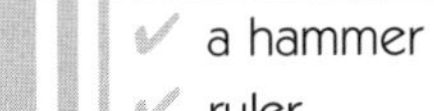

You need:

- a hammer
- ruler
- loop of string
- table

THE ILLUSTRATION SHOWS HOW YOU CAN build an odd structure that will balance on the edge of a table.

Tie the ends of a length of string, then twist the string into loops until it resembles a bracelet made of string. The picture shows how this "bracelet" is used to keep the end of a ruler attached to the end of a hammer's handle. Place the other end of the ruler on the edge of a table as shown. The structure will remain balanced even though it seems as if the hammer's heavy head would make the structure fall to the floor.

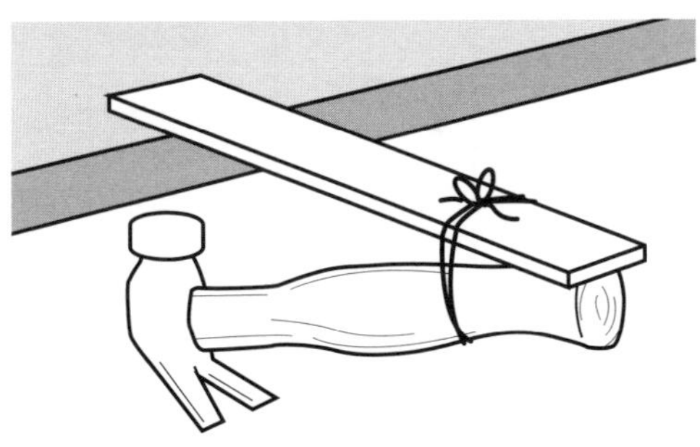

### Why does it work?

The hammer's heavy head shifts the system's center of gravity to a point slightly under the table's edge.

# 94

# THE RISING HOURGLASS

A POPULAR SCIENCE TOY SOLD IN FRANCE CONSISTS OF A GLASS cylinder completely filled with water and sealed at both ends. At the top of the cylinder floats an hourglass with sand in its lower compartment (Figure 1).

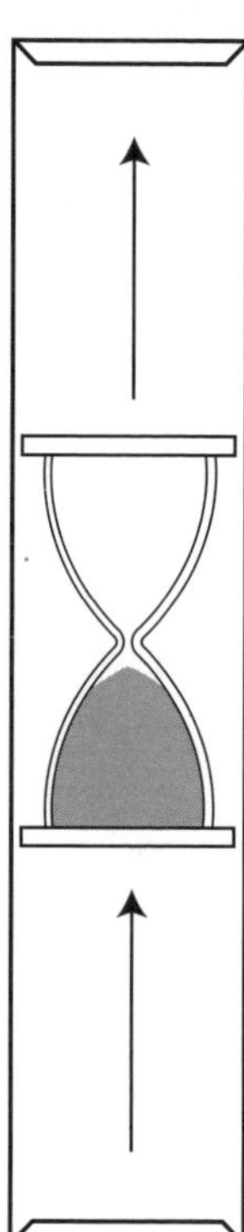

When you invert the cylinder (Figure 2), the hourglass stays at the bottom until almost all its sand has gone down. When this happens, the hourglass mysteriously rises to the top (Figure 3).

Why should a change in the sand's location alter the weight of the hourglass?

This is very puzzling, especially to physicists.

## The Secret:

The secret is subtle. The hourglass has a circumference that is almost, but not quite the same as the cylinder's circumference. When the hourglass is at the bottom, the sand in its top portion tips the hourglass imperceptibly. This causes it to touch the side of the cylinder. There is just enough friction created to prevent the hourglass from rising until the falling sand reaches its lower part, causing the hourglass to become upright. When it no longer touches the side of the cylinder, the friction vanishes, allowing the hourglass to float to the top.

# 95

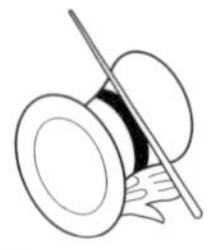

# A BALANCING FEAT

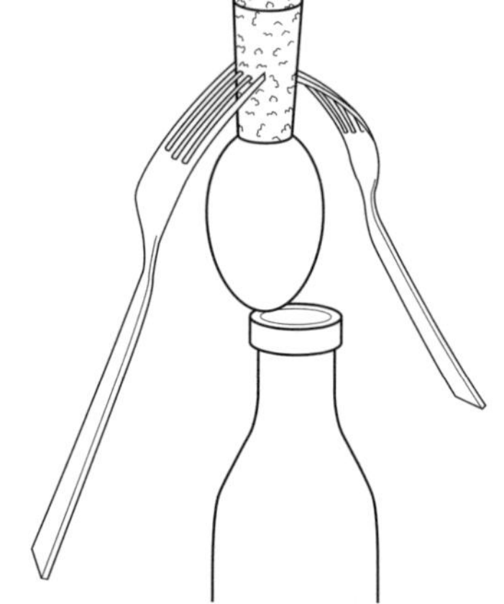

You need:

- a cork ✓
- a hard-boiled egg ✓
- 2 forks ✓
- a bottle with a flat rim opening ✓

THIS STUNT IS DESCRIBED IN MANY NINETEENTH- CENTURY books ON recreational science. The picture is self explanatory. The bottle's opening must have a flat rim, and the bottom of the cork must be cut to make it sufficiently concave to fit snugly on the egg's end.

## Why does it work?

The center of gravity is that point at which the entire weight of an object is evenly balanced. For example, if you were to attach two weights, a one-pound weight and a two-pound weight, to different ends of a broom handle, the center of gravity would be much closer to the two pound weight—it would be the point at which you could balance the broomstick in your hand. So the center of gravity is not necessarily at the spatial center of an object. In fact, for an object that has a very irregular shape it might not even be a point on or in the object itself!

# Index

## About the Author

WORLD FAMOUS AS THE PUZZLE MASTER WHO WROTE THE "Mathematical Games" column of Scientific American magazine for 25 years, Martin Gardner has also written close to 70 books on such subjects as science (including a book that Time magazine called "by far the most lucid explanation of Einstein's theories"), mathematics, philosophy, religion, poetry, literary criticism (including The Annotated Alice, a classic examination of Alice in Wonderland that is still selling large numbers of copies now, more than 30 years after it was first published), and, of course, puzzles (out of 29 puzzle books for adults and children, only one is out of print!).

The son of an Oklahoma wildcat oil prospector, Gardner attended the University of Chicago, where he received a degree in philosophy. After graduation he worked on the Tulsa (Oklahoma) Tribune. He sold his first story to Esquire, published articles on logic and math in specialist magazines and became a contributing editor to Humpty Dumpty's Magazine before starting his legendary column.

Martin Gardner has had a lifelong passion for conjuring, and many of his original magic tricks have become classics among magicians.

Dubbed "The Magician of Math" by *Newsweek*, Martin Gardner, now retired, makes his home in North Carolina, where he continues to amaze his fans with more and more books, articles, and ideas.